THE HIDDEN PRINCESS

"And they shall be mine, saith the Lord of hosts, in that day when I make up my *jewels*; and I will spare them, as a man spareth his own son that serveth him."
Malachi 3:17

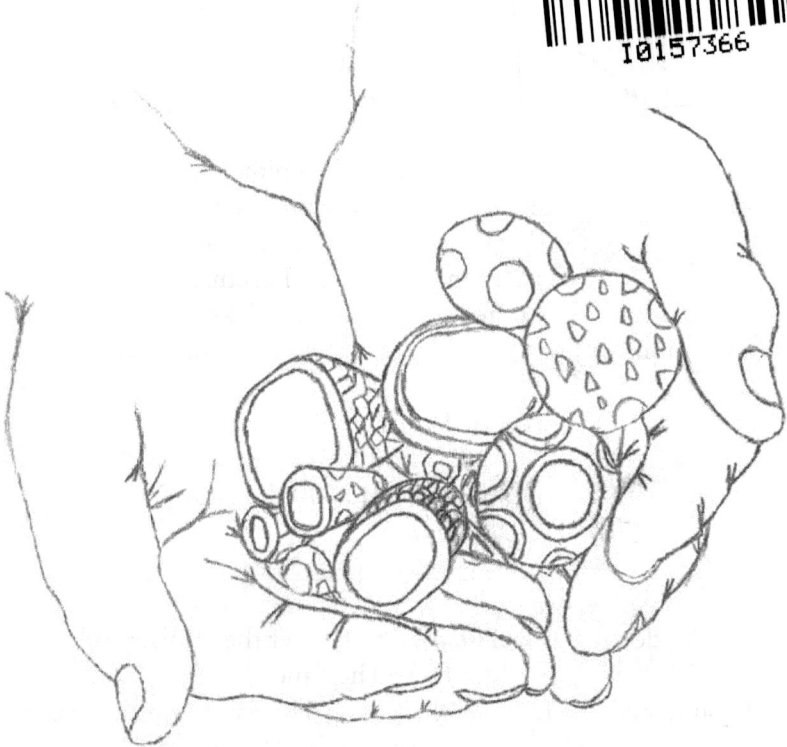

The Hidden Princess
Published by Itza God Thing Publishing© 2014
"Itza God Thing Publishing" publishes spiritual music
and books serving the ministry in spreading the work of God.
All rights reserved
Jewel's In The Sand Ministry© is a non-profit 501c3 ministry
"Healing The Wounded" through the Word of God.
Encouraging and teaching those who choose to live a life of
victory and freedom from internal and physical pain.
A healing that can only come from God.
Author Rev. Debra Ann Sutterfield
With contributions by Donna Lee Story, Cecilia Karlene Smith
and
Amber McKenzie Smith
Edited by Nicole B. Medeiros
Cover design by Jeffery Lockington Jr.
Cover design by Grayson Foreman
Illustrated by Dylan Hendricks
Donations to Jewel's In The Sand Ministry can be made to:

Jewels In The Sand Ministry©
PO Box 194
Lexington, Mo 64067
or
www.jewelsinthesand.org

All donations will be used to further the ministry of
Jewel's In The Sand
If you would like to have "Jewel's In The Sand" speak at your
church you may contact the Ministry at
www.info@jewelsinthesand.org

All scriptures used are from the Holy Bible KJV unless
otherwise noted

Acknowledgements

First of all I would like to thank my loving husband Phillip. You stood by my side during the trials of the ministry and the writing of this book. God has blessed me with such an encourager as you tolerated the moments of insanity. You cooked, cleaned and did laundry while constantly encouraging me to see this project to completion. Thank you!

I would like to acknowledge and thank the following people who have been responsible in influencing me in my spiritual growth.

Betty and Frank Therber for hearing God's voice calling for me before I knew I would end up in a ministry, for supplying me with spiritual wisdom, encouragement and sowing seeds into "Jewel's In The Sand" and for teaching me how to forgive.

Thanks to my armor bearer Donna Story who always has my back and her contributions to the Hidden Princess and Cecilia Smith my business developer for her vision, support and contributions to The Hidden Princess.

Thank you to Nicole B. Medeiros for the hours of editing and your contribution to the ministry and to Jeffrey Lockington Jr for working with us until he had the perfect cover. Thanks to Grayson Foreman for staying up all night to assist me with last minute changes and to Dylan Hendricks for the great illustration.

A special thanks to Pastor's Leonard and Darla Hendricks for their constant support, prayers and encouragement in both the ministry and my personal life

I am so blessed to call you all "friend".

A special thanks to my mom, who never gave up on me. I love you Mom!

This book is dedicated to my children Amber and Mack for teaching me to love. As I have dedicated my life to raising you I had to learn to heal, forgive and break generational curses. In loving you I began to realize the true sacrifice God made for me in allowing His own Son to suffer and die for my salvation.

Table of Contents

How To Use The Book

This book may be used alone or in a Jewels In The Sand group. It was designed to help you become a greater you. The you, that God purposed for His glory. Though this is a short book it holds a lot of power designed to empower you. Read it slow and apply it to your life step by step. Master one step before moving to another. This is not a quick fix, you must work through it. When you feel it doesn't apply to you dig in and study, it's for you. My hopes and those of the contributors of the book are to show you that you are not alone. Our pains and struggles are real life experiences. We pray that you will use this as a work book and apply the lessons and scriptures to your life. Growing is never painless, it often opens old wounds but to find victory you must scratch the word die out of depression (~~depression~~) and press-on.

Our earnest hope is that you will eventually use your experiences to help others heal and lead them to salvation.

We can do all things through Christ who strengthens us, but nothing by ourselves. If you have been struggling and not being able to fix anything or anybody I implore you to begin with you.

May God bless you on your journey.

Rev. Debra Ann Sutterfield

About The Authors

During our journey of writing this book I came to know some phenomenal women. These women have been joined together by God. They have all become my friends.

One Sunday after preaching and while standing in a prayer line a small but mighty warrior stepped out of the prayer line and pointed her finger at me saying "I don't know what it is but God is putting us together to do a mighty work for Him". I had never met Cecilia Smith before that but scheduled to have dinner with her. You will see how God has used her in the chapters "Broken to Beauty" and "How Does Your Garden Grow". She is now working in the ministry by my side as my friend and business developer, I am very Blessed to have her.

Donna Story is a mighty prayer warrior who attends church with me. She stepped into the ministry as support and has since become a major part of the ministry as my "armor bearer". Read how God moved the impossible mountain of un-forgiveness out of her life in her chapters "As We Speak" and "Believing in God's Love". Her testimony is very powerful in forgiveness.

The chapter "Yes, I Am A Princess" ended up being the chapter that decided the title of the book. Not because of whom she is but because of the testimony she wrote which moved the entire ministry team. While she is not an active part of the ministry she wanted to add something to the book. I am glad I gave her the opportunity because it added yet another testimony that touched me in quiet a different way. You see, the author of "Yes, I Am A Princess" is Amber McKenzie Smith, she is not only my friend she is my daughter whom I love more than life.

Breaking generational curses is a very determined and difficult step but necessary to lead yourself and your children to victory.

I am Debra Ann Sutterfield and a very Blessed woman to be able to serve with these mighty women of God!

THE HIDDEN PRINCESS

Rev. Debra Ann Sutterfield

With contributions by
Donna Lee Story
Cecilia Karlene Smith
And
Amber McKenzie Smith

A Jewel's In The Sand Ministry Book
Itza God Thing Publishing
Lexington, Mo
2014

THE HIDDEN PRINCESS

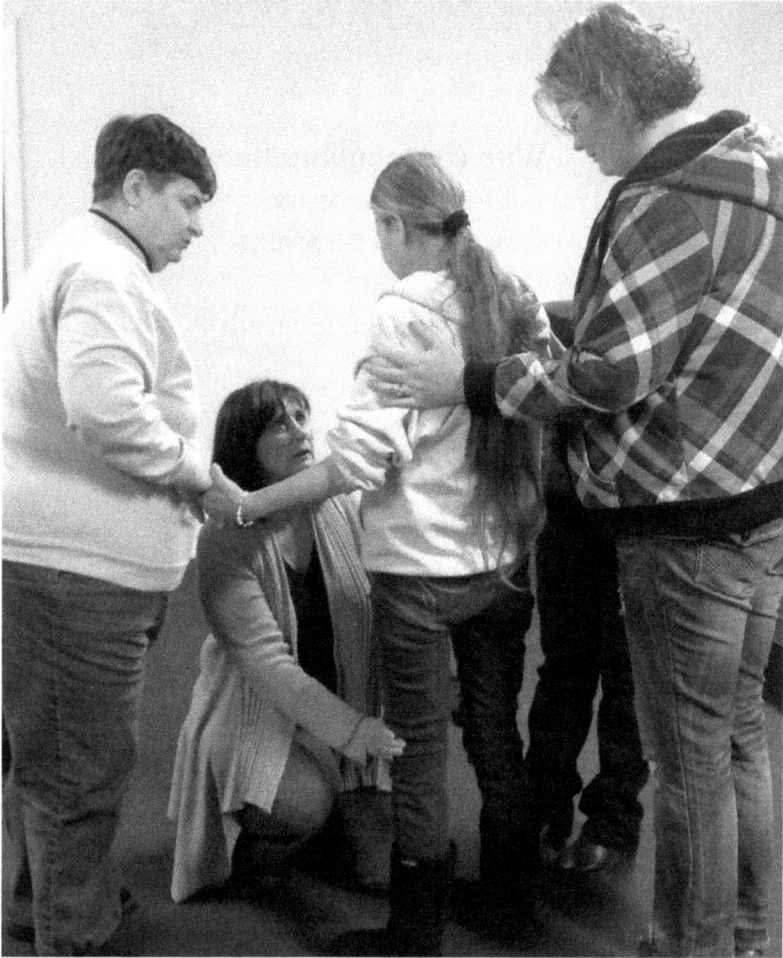

Chapter 1

You Can't Unscramble That Egg!

By Debra Ann Sutterfield

"We can't change where we have been or what we have done, but we can change where we are going and how we will do it."

You Can't Unscramble That Egg

Writing your own story should be easy instead it has been a challenge for me. I have procrastinated and put off the inevitable. But, here I sit, facing my past and the person I was. I always refer to my past as "in my last life," because my past is so totally different than my life today. Today "I am" positive, confident and happy, "I am" a leader, and a preacher, "I am"!

Everyone has a past. Everyone has suffered pain. My story is no different. I share my story to show you the effects from both sides, the victim and the victorious, because I have been both. For so many years of my life, I walked in defeat, I couldn't figure out why God didn't love me, why my husband didn't love me, why I was always treated so bad. Why, God, why? God revealed to me that I was one cracked egg! It turns out we are all cracked eggs; some have worse cracks than others.

We all have pain from our past. It doesn't really matter what caused the pain. I have learned one pain is no different than another the cause may differ but the pain remains the same. The way we deal with our pain is what determines the life we live, the person we become. No matter where you are you can change the path of defeat, depression and the lack of joy to become the person you wish you could be.

Now, read on and get to know that cracked egg named Debra Ann and see how I found victory, joy and peace and how I discovered a me that I am able to love.

As you read through you will meet three other amazing women who also found happiness through the lessons found inside this book.

3

You Can't Unscramble That Egg!

When I was born, my parents were much too young to start a family. The day I was born, my mom had turned seventeen just one week before. I wasn't even two-years-old when my sister was born. At age four, another sister came along, and at age five, yet another sister. Two months before I was eight, my brother was born. Yes, by the time my mother was twenty five she had given birth to five children.

We all are born with a shell of protection around us, perfect little eggs, but the shell itself is fragile. When I was born, life began like every other baby the world was all about me. I was the center of attention. I was a happy bubbly baby, cute, and smart, too! (Ok, it's my story so I get to tell it my way.) In all seriousness, though, as I began grow, so did the tension in my home. My mom and dad began to argue, and Daddy began to drink. The loud voices, angry tones, and slamming doors hurt and led to a crack in my shell. I didn't understand what was happening around me, but there was a feeling of fear. Of course since the world was all about me, it must be my fault somehow.

The drinking became worse, and the angry words were louder as I worked harder to make everyone happy. If I kept the other children quiet, if I could get Daddy everything he needed, if I could make my Mommy not cry then it would be okay. Days turned to weeks, months and years. When I was four, Daddy lost his sister, her husband, and their three-month-old baby in a tragic fire that stole many lives in our neighborhood. Daddy had been angry and not speaking to his sister when she died, he now buried his feelings in the bottle. The more he drank, the more violent he became, the more cracks this egg had in my shell. Daddy was so unhappy, hurt and wounded. At the time, I didn't know that he was a cracked egg, too, because, in my eyes, it was all about me.

When I was eight, I was now in the war. I fought every day to make things work. There was no room for any mistakes, no room for forgiveness or a second chance. I realize now that I was walking on eggshells, my own egg shells. You see, the cracks had become so severe that now I was laying exposed to the world, my shell shattered. I now was a "scrambled egg." Daddy would rip off his belt or pick up part of a rubber hose or a fan belt and beat you with it. You never knew what would trigger the anger. Yes, I was walking on eggshells, my own eggshells. I would try to diffuse problems before they began. If my siblings did things that tilted Daddy, I would try to take the beating for them.

My Mom was a cracked egg too. She had to deal with her own anger and depression. I remember all five of us got the measles, and before the last one was healed, we started coming down with chickenpox. Mom became so exhausted that she collapsed and had to be hospitalized. I was terrified of losing my mom; my stress level was so high at the age of eight, I was hospitalized with migraine headaches.

The war in my home was so chaotic that I was more scrambled daily. Many nights I would climb out of bed, go get my siblings, and put them in my bed. Then I would go into the living room or kitchen, or where ever the fight was. I would often jump onto Daddy's back and try to pull him off of Momma. We had holes in the walls of our house where he had lost his temper and punched them. It only made sense that eventually it would be a person who would be punched. It is really sad, as my dad was such a brilliant man, he could build anything with his hands.

While other friends could spend the night out, no one wanted to spend the night at my house and I didn't want them there, either. My social life was pretty limited in friendships, but I knew enough that my friend's homes weren't stressed like ours was. When I was eight, I had the greatest Christmas of my life. Santa brought me my best friend. I woke up Christmas morning before daylight and under the tree was a saddle! I ran and jumped in the middle of Daddy and Momma's bed ecstatic. I didn't care if I got a beating; nothing could mess this up. Daddy got up and went out and saddled my pony "Rusty." From that day, when I got upset, stressed out, overwhelmed, I would saddle Rusty and ride out into the woods. Sometimes we just rode, sometimes I would get off and lean next to a tree and tell him my worries as he ate acorns. I would sit there and pray and ask God for my daddy not to drink. Usually I would stay in the woods too long and couldn't find my way out because it had grown dark. I would lay the reigns down on Rusty's neck and say "Rusty, take me home." With Rusty, I could escape from reality into a world where I was a Princess, but I would always have to return to reality.

Rage was a normal thing in our home, but our mom taught us that we weren't supposed to let people know. It was a secret! When we went to church,

Momma would tell us to "stand up straight, no one knows what goes on in our home." I remember, to this day, hearing those "sweet Christian Ladies (?)," as we walked by say, "there goes Gail and those pitiful little children." I tried to hold my head up and be proud, but now I had been titled as "pitiful." They tell us, "sticks and stones will break your bones, but words will never hurt you." Well. let me just say this, my bones would heal and grow back. Those words pierce through your heart, and to this day, I remember the pain. I guess "those pitiful children" were the first words that I remember as forming who I would become. I heard them, but I couldn't decide if my mom heard them and ignored them. Maybe she couldn't hear that well, maybe she is just nuts and living in a make believe world. It didn't matter what the reason, I wasn't going to be the one that burst that bubble of hers.

My world was just getting more scrambled and confused all of the time. I loved my daddy, but he became more and more someone I didn't know. I learned to be able to tell if he was drinking by the way his hair laid on his head, the way he moved, and the way he walked. We spent more and more time out of the house and away from Daddy, it was just safer. Daddy's violence became worse - more alcohol, more drunken rages which escalated to Momma's anger and depression, more fights between Mom and Dad we had to witness. It was not unusual to see Mom wearing a turtleneck sweater on a hot summer day to cover the choke marks from the night before.

The day came where hands and fists were not enough Daddy, the daddy of five little children, held a pistol between Momma's eyes and said "you've got to die." Mom asked "what about the children?" Daddy said, "they have to die, we all have to die." Somehow she was able to calm him into wanting to talk to his momma, but it was the beginning of impending death. Months later he shot himself in the side, amazingly, he survived. Our world had reached a place that I couldn't understand. I began to respond in the moment of crisis like an oiled machine. I would hide the children and prepare for battle.

When I was thirteen my Dad came home drunk again. My Mom had a salon behind our house, and she was there working with a couple of clients. Daddy told me to go get Mom, which I did. We didn't want him in the salon. I sat in the salon while she went to the house to pacify Daddy. As I sat there talking with her clients, I had a fear grip me and knew instantly something was wrong. I got up and ran straight for the house. When I got there, Daddy had Momma held against the back door choking her, I couldn't get in. I took a deep breath and cried out, "Jesus, help me!" I hit the door, and they both hit the floor. I jumped on top of Daddy, screaming, punching and kicking for all I could. Mom gathered the other kids and told them to get in the car. She yelled at me to get in the car as all of the drama unfolded into a nightmarish event. Clients with curlers in their hair were running for their cars as they were spinning wheels to get out of the driveway. My Daddy showed up with his pistols, he aimed one right at my little brother's head. Mom snatched him out of the way, and the shots began to ring as Daddy walked around the car, shooting out all of our tires.

I'm so confused. This can't be right. Why, God? I keep praying to you, why God? How do things go so wrong? God, aren't we your children? My emotions are so scrambled and beaten. Is it not hard enough being a teenager? My mom was now an island alone in her own world. My siblings and I had to figure out how to grow up with no leadership. Daddy was arrested for that event, and they divorced, but it didn't mean sanity. Daddy was later found on our roof with a spear gun and Mom's name tied to it. Do people really live like this? "You mean, they don't?" This helps you understand my scrambled egg mentality, doesn't it? I was an angry, angry person. I began my life of un-forgiveness and not being able to trust anyone. How can you trust people? The ones who were responsible for my safety were the very ones I couldn't trust with it.

At fifteen I began dating the person I would marry at the age of sixteen. I loved him with all that I was. He was my knight in shining armor, the one who would take me away from the insanity and take me to a safe haven. There was, however, a small flaw in my dream world. My knight in shining armor was (you guessed it) a cracked egg. He, too, had grown up in a totally dysfunctional home. Now you have two scrambled eggs trying to do things they had no idea how to do, love each other. It seems like that would come naturally, but the only thing that came naturally was the arguing. That part, as painful as it was, became the one thing we excelled in. He called me names. My parents hadn't done that, but those ladies in church had called us pitiful. Maybe I was what he was calling me. Why would he lie to me? He did love me, didn't he? So as the years went by, I became the person he described me to be, one of which was worthless. Oh, it's not his fault, he is as scrambled as I am and I became a

10

"victim" along the way. I started life as a perfect little egg without a crack and the world was all about me. Now, the world is all about poor, pitiful me and my scrambled up emotions.

I was married twelve years feeling all sorry for me because I didn't deserve any better when God blessed me with the most precious gift of a perfect little egg, my daughter. Now finally, someone who would love me just like I am. Now you can see a perfect storm brewing, but I couldn't. Here are two broken people about to embark on raising a perfect little jewel. How badly could we screw this up? My entire world was wrapped up in loving this baby and raising the perfect child. I was involved in trying to make my life perfect through her.

Five years later another perfect baby was born, this one a son. I praised God for my blessings and the miracles he had given me. I continued to try to work hard not to be worthless in my husband's eyes, doing everything he needed for his business, cooking, cleaning etc. and being the perfect uptight and over the top Mommy. I was over-protective, afraid God would remove the blessings he had bestowed unto me. My husband had become distant and disconnected from the children and me. When we were together, he didn't speak, or we were yelling at each other. I remember, one day, as the two children sat on the sofa, we were yelling. When I turned to walk off with tears flowing, I saw them with their hands over their ears, and pain went through my heart.

I began to analyze my life that had spiraled out of control. That is laughable - when had there ever been control? I was depressed, thought of suicide, and filled with anger and bitterness. I don't know why these things happen to me. What have I done to deserve this? Yep, I was a victim, 100% victim. Poor little me. I was not accepting responsibility for one thing in my life. I spent every day of my life crying. I decided, after twenty one years of marriage, to leave this man. His armor was not shining so bright. He had become a wicked knight.

I really and truly believed that he would realize how important I was and come get me. He filed for a divorce instead. Shock. I really was worthless to him. Now for the reality check. I was damaged goods. I had no self-worth. I was a victim. I was one seriously scrambled egg! What can you do with a scrambled egg? With the right ingredients, you can bake a cake! It was time for me to look at my life and see if I could do anything to change who I was.

God is so good to us. If we allow Him to work in our life and ask for His guidance, miraculous things begin to happen. I left and moved to Nashville. I was scared to death. I met a lady named Frieda who saw potential in me. She inspired me to better myself and apply myself. I became an educator for a product company and a motivational speaker. I began to feel a bit empowered. I was no longer crying myself to sleep at night. I met a man who became my second husband. He told me such beautiful things about myself. I used to come home at night and say "lie to me baby, I like it a lot." I realized that the words we believe and say about ourselves are who we become.

The Bible says in Proverbs 23:7 as a man thinketh in his heart so is he. I was thinking garbage in my heart, and that was what I became. The great news is that we can change who we are and what we are by changing the way we think and the words we use. It takes determination and the desire to overcome. You see, I made a decision to break this generational curse that was in my family. My precious gifts God had blessed me with deserved much more than I was capable of giving them. Today, my daughter and son are grown up, they are confident and secure in who they are. They are full of joy and laughter. I continue to be proud of them as they turned out to be wonderful people despite the mother they began life with. I believe, if you ask them today, they will agree that God used one scrambled egg and added the perfect ingredients to bake the perfect cake for our family.

You see, we all started out little eggs without blemish, but as we go through life, cracks happen. You can't change your past and what you have experienced. You can't unscramble that egg. But, you can add the ingredients to sweeten your life. As we say in Jewels In The Sand, "you can't unscramble that egg but you can bake cake."

Notes

On this page take the time to examine how you may relate to the chapter you have just read. How will you be able to utilize the points made in this chapter? How will you apply them to your actions and your daily decisions? In healing, it is so important to stop lying to yourself. Be honest, this is between you and God. Remember God loves you, no matter what you believe. If you will be honest with yourself you will be healed by applying these simple but painful truths to your life. Don't give up push through!

_____

_____

_____

_____

_____

_____

_____

_____

_____

_____

_____

_____

_____

_____

_____

_____

_____

_____

_____

_____

_____

_____

Chapter 2

The Choice Is Yours

By Debra Ann Sutterfield

Choose my instruction instead of silver, knowledge rather than
choice gold,
[11] for wisdom is more precious than rubies, and nothing you desire
can compare with her.
Proverbs 8:10-11 New International Version (NIV)

It takes time to heal, but more than time, it takes a decision. You must decide to take the challenge. You must decide to go through the process. A decision is a choice and the choice is yours. We realize the pain you will go through, because we have gone through the same healing process. Many emotions take place, you want to run, you want to quit, you want to blame, but whatever you feel, **if** you want to heal, you must press on. This isn't easy, but is the treasure on the other side worth the work or the pain? I can tell you from my own experience, it is indeed. To finally hold my head high, knowing I have been set free, is something I could not go pick up from a store.

During the healing process, we have found most everyone reaches a point that is almost unbearable to face. We all come to the wall of pain where we want to just throw up our hands in defeat and run to our old safe place we have created. The safe place may be in the form of anger, rage, depression, fear or any other variety of emotions we have created that has become our haven. Once again, we are forced to realize these emotions we use to protect ourselves is not a friend or safe haven, they are lies we use to escape freedom. They are the prison we choose to remain in.

Instead of making the choice to change our behavior, we tend to choose to punish ourselves. Often we use self-abuse or self-destruction tactics to ease the pain. These tactics can include, but is not limited to, food indulgence, drugs, alcohol, self- mutilation, sexual promiscuity, gambling, bad relationships and many others. I have heard for years about marathon runners running so hard and long, and then they hit a wall.

Runners say it is like they cannot take another step. The human body feels like it weighs a ton and the very effort to move another muscle seems impossible. It is in this moment of the most difficult battle that the runner has to dig deep inside of them, and against every human effort, they connect with an inner strength, an almost supernatural strength, to press on. They say that the energy that comes after the breakthrough becomes almost effortless and easy.

Just like the runners, when we hit that wall of pain where we want to quit and give up, if we dig deep inside ourselves to the true Supernatural, we too will feel an effortless breakthrough. Like the runner we can finish the race victoriously. When we dig deep inside of us we realize there is one crucial element that is necessary to be successful in our journey to become victorious. That element is God! We should know that through the life, crucifixion, and resurrection of Jesus Christ, we are worthy of breaking all chains of bondage against our soul. Christ now acts as an intercessory for our forgiveness and prayer requests. **But** the choice is yours.

As we go through the process of healing, if you do not know Jesus as your Lord and Savior, and if you seek the healing and peace only He can give, I invite you to contact a Christian leader and tell them you want to invite Jesus into your heart. Your leader will gladly and without judgment lead you into salvation and a peace that surpasses all human understanding. Healing is, indeed, up to you. What has happened to you was out of your control, but, today, you can choose to change that. The choice is yours. You can decide today to grow, to change, to become a new person; you can decide to leave the past behind, to quit being the victim and start living victoriously.

Whatever you choose is your decision and a choice that **you** have to make. This will be your own journey; it's nothing that anyone can do for you or any trip that anyone can take for you. This is your personal journey, to heal and to move on. We have lived in our past for so long not knowing that there was an option or a decision we could make to change where we were, what we were doing, and how we were doing it. Looking at our life from a different angle, we may have never recognized that we had a problem. I forever thought I was right and nobody understood me. I now realize I had it backwards. I was wrong, others wanted to understand and love me, but I had a "victim mentality." I praise God for giving me the victory of removing the self-serving scales of deceit I had over my eyes. The eyes of my soul are now clear.

Yes, my past caused me a lot of pain, and I walked around pretending I was happy and strong, but nothing could be further from the truth. There were days I didn't open my drapes or the blinds in my house, I was having a pity party, and you were not invited. The only personal invitations were between me and my old friend, depression. Once a dear friend of mine asked me why I kept my blinds closed some days. She had noticed them when she would drive by. When I told her it was because I was suffering from depression on those days, she said next time she saw my blinds closed, she was going to stop and see me. I instantly regretted what I had told her. You see, I just wanted to spend that time alone with my old friend depression. Janet loved me and wanted to help me. I wanted to be left alone to wallow in misery. I was making a choice to not heal, there was no light at the end of my tunnel.

It is said the definition of insanity is doing the same thing over and over again expecting different results. We, the victims, of our past continually are hurt by others. We try so hard to make someone love us by trying to earn their love or appreciation. We may be trying to force our husbands to love us by being the best housekeeper, the best cook, maybe, by being control freaks. When, in reality, we can't control the monster inside of us, the monster that creates the pain inside of us. Maybe, the saddest thing, is that the monster becomes our friend, it is the one emotion we can depend on. My monster was two-headed, one named rage, the other un-forgiveness. My rage came from the inability to control my surroundings and the constant degrading remarks made by my husband. Before that, it was my lack of control in an alcoholic home.

My un-forgiveness came from building what I referred to as a wall of protection. If you hurt me, I would not give you that opportunity again. That was a lie I was telling myself. I was working in the perfect will of Satan, calling myself a Christian. I was ignorant! Oh, but wait, doesn't the Bible say in Hosea 4:6, *my people are destroyed for lack of knowledge?* I was walking the perfect walk of destruction. Not realizing I was in bondage, in prison and the entire time, I held the keys to open the jail cell and freely walk out.

You see, Jesus paid that price for our freedom, yours and mine. So, we sit under the oppression in a cell of our own choice. We sit secluded, separated, and alone. But, because God has given me the vision by removing the scales from my eyes and shattering the chains I sat in, I am able to share my story that led me to be set free with you. Maybe, you will choose the path to that same victory. That is, if you want to be free. If you want to lay down fear, oppression, and depression, take it to the foot of the Cross.

In making a choice to gain your freedom, you need to know that we cannot change others. Change is a choice you can make for you, but you cannot make that choice for someone else. You cannot change your spouse, your children, or your friends. Many times our children, spouse, or friends begin to see a change in us, and in hearing the words of blessings you speak over them, they start small steps of change in themselves. You can set an example of what change you have made in you, which encourages others to want the same. But, once again, I tell you, this change is about changing you, how you think, speak and respond in situations that tend to trigger emotions. This change and choice is about you! If your change affects those around you in a positive way, what a blessing, but the change is a choice for you.

I have seen women join the group then try to force their children into the same mindset because of their personal victory. I must warn you, each and every person has a personal breakthrough on their own, in their own moment. Don't beg and plead - just walk the path God has lit so brilliantly for you to follow. Pray for your family and your friends. This journey is for you! The harder you push someone, the more they push back. Walk your own walk at your own pace. In one of our groups, two different ladies had decided to leave their husbands. I let them know this group cannot change others, only you. I asked them if they would take the challenge to stick it out for a while and work on how they reacted in situations that triggered their pain. The ladies agreed they would try. I was in a "Jewels In The Sand" group meeting with them a few weeks later and both of these same ladies were just bubbling over with how their husbands have changed. We have to understand the change is internal in how we view things and how we respond to things. But, probably the most important step would be the positive words of blessings we speak over ourselves, our spouse, and our children. Make sure your blessings are positive and have no negative words attached (you have a beautiful smile, how can you be so mean?). When we phrase our words so pointedly, we cancel the positive with the negative. Our minds will forever remember the negative, not the positive. Our spouses give us compliments along the way, but we hang on to the negative words, which cancel out the good. We have to choose to speak blessings rather than curses.

Proverbs 18:21
Death and life are in the power of the tongue: and they that love it shall eat the fruit thereof.

When making a choice, choose life. Your words can bless, and you will reap the blessings. Or, your words can curse, and you will reap the curses. It is amazing what happens when you go through life looking daily for someone to bless. Soon blessings begin to come to you. But, don't do it for that reason, do it because you truly want to bless others as you wish to be blessed. If we start moving in small steps, we will soon feel the positive reaction caused by our positive action. We can change our situation by choosing first to change.

It is not easy to realize the problem is us. I remember, one day, I was really upset with Phillip. On my way to work that morning, on Christian Radio, I heard a sermon on love, I said "man this is good stuff, Phillip should be hearing this!" Then, as luck would have it, the next sermon was on marriage. Yep, Phillip should be hearing this. I left work on a break to run some paperwork over to our district office and a talk show was on, you guessed it, marriage! I wish Phillip was hearing this. After work that evening, another sermon on love and another on marriage! "Man, I wish Phillip was hearing this." Then I heard it! That small voice of God quietly saying, "I didn't give it to Phillip, I gave it to you."

It's easy to lay blame on someone else and difficult to admit we are the ones at fault. I am so strong-willed, always wanting to be the one that is right, always wanting to be the wronged one, the victim. The truth is, I have to make a choice to change my behavior, if I want to see change, to become healthy, and find joy. So how do I begin to make that change when I am so beat up and so weak? I choose to ask Jesus to assist me in making me a better me.

Philippians 4:11
I can do __all__ things through Christ who strengthens me.

God is so willing to forgive us, we are the ones who harbor un-forgiveness. If we allow God to lead us, we will grow, blossom and achieve great things. Our families will change and grow closer, not because they were changed, but because we have. We change through choosing to take control of our lives and allowing Jesus to place peace in our heart.

Psalms 51:*10*
Create in me a clean heart, O God; and renew a right spirit within me.

There is such a great life ahead for you, if you choose to make the change. Happiness is a choice. Love is a choice. Salvation is a choice. Anyone who has ever suffered from depression is aware that thoughts of death will always pop into our minds. Satan loves to trap us in that area, in depression. I learned something a few years ago about depression. If you take the word depression and scratch out the word die ~~depression,~~ you are left with "press on." Are you willing to make the choice and "press on?"

We have to learn a different path to walk, a different way to speak, and different reactions when our buttons are pushed. This is all a choice for healing. Every day our life takes a new turn, we never know what challenge life is going to throw at us, but we can go through with dignity and character, if we choose to.

For so many years, we have responded to things with the same behavior, without control, we just react. It is time to choose to follow the lead of God - to live through the wisdom of Proverbs, applying your heart to understanding, hearing the words of wisdom, choosing to improve your life. It is better to avoid arguing and answer softly, living a life of godliness.

Proverbs 2:2
So that thou incline thine ear unto wisdom, and apply thine heart to understanding;

1 Timothy 3:16
And without controversy great is the mystery of godliness:

Titus 2:12
Teaching us that, denying ungodliness and worldly lusts, we should live soberly, righteously, and godly, in this present world;

It's time to break all generational curses against you and your children. Take authority over your life. Jesus has given us the authority to cancel the curses in our lives. So, the question is, do you truly want change in your life? Do you want it enough to work for it, retraining yourself and your behavior, in action, reactions and words? Making the right choices can change your life. It takes you from self- destruction to the path of healing. Yes, it's work, but the results will be dynamic.

Choosing
Healing
Over
Insults
Consistently
Effectively
Successfully
(CHOICES)

BEHAVIORAL CHOICES

Do you recognize the difference in good behavior and bad? In this day and age we have come to expect bad as good and good as bad that we have a hard time knowing what is true. Here is a list of behaviors that you may compare to how you think or live:

<u>GOOD</u>

Exhibits responsibility in daily routine at home, work & socially.

Balances hard work and fulfillment of obligations with recreation.

Shows genuine consideration to others.

Earns respect of others & self-respect through achievement.

Urges to violate arise then disappears with little effort.

Shows respect for the right & property of others.

Values opinions and judgment of others.

Makes choices for the good of others & self.

<u>BAD</u>

Acts semi-responsible, voicing many excuses.

Routinely lies, manipulates, and intimidates in an unbalanced lifestyle.

Habitually inconsiderate, unreliably late.

Prone to procrastination, laziness, and poor work/study habits.

Fails to fulfill intentions, promises and obligations.

Exhibits excellent behavior only when immediate benefits are at hand.

Puts authorities against each other.

Makes apathetic, incomplete attempts & excuses to fail.

Lacks goals or direction.

Do you live your life in any of these behaviors? If you do your life is out of control and may lead to some serious consequences. Listed below is some **examples**

of really bad behavior and offset underneath each behavior is the **extreme of that behavior:**

Bad behavior: Acts responsibly only if there is no alternative & resists even then.
    Extremely bad behavior: Accepts no responsibility.

Bad behavior: Acts secretive & prefers to be a loner, considering yourself better than others.
    Extremely bad behavior: Commits crimes, uses alcohol & other drugs to feel better.

Bad behavior: Closed & unreceptive of other's views.
    Extremely bad behavior: Exhibits no consideration for others.

Bad behavior: Feels successful because offenses/crimes have gone undetected.
    Extremely bad behavior: Overconfident, arrogant, continues against all odds to try to "beat the system."

Bad behavior: When consequences or restraints are removed, will commit violations previously only imagined.
    Extremely bad behavior: Continually plots and focuses on selfish/criminal thoughts.

Bad behavior: Appears responsible & surprises many when caught in a serious offense.
    Extremely bad behavior: Makes decisions without regard for others or consideration of

consequences.

Bad behavior: Enjoys using anger to intimidate & get own way.

      Extremely bad behavior: Views self as a "good person" while ignoring harm done to others. Sees being nice as a weakness.

Bad behavior: Choose to move away to gain greater freedom & avoid detection.

      Extremely bad behavior: Exploits relationships for self-profit. Promotes self at the expense of others.

Bad behavior: Active in minor offenses or crimes without detection. Strong urges to violate others but you are restrained only by fearing the consequences of being caught.

      Extremely bad behavior: Cries "unfair", claims injustice and blames others.

      As you read the Bible remember these behavioral choices and see what God's Word speaks to you.

ACRONYMS

We would like to share with you a few special words we have either heard or have made up ourselves into an acronym. God has placed such a special blessing on words and we need to be careful how we speak and use them. These are just a little food for thought.

We exterminate all ANTS
A-any
N-negative
TS-thoughts

Let me give you some HUGS
H-helping
U-us
G-grow
S-spiritually

What is FEAR?
F-false
E-expectations
A-appearing
R-real

Making the right CHOICES can change your life.
C-choosing
H-healing
O-over
I-insults
C-consistently and
E-effectively
S-successfully!

Have some fun and make up some acronyms of your own that may help you to remember some important life applications.

Notes

On this page take the time to examine how you may relate to the chapter you have just read. How will you be able to utilize the points made in this chapter? How will you apply them to your actions and your daily decisions? In healing, it is so important to stop lying to yourself. Be honest, this is between you and God. Remember God loves you, no matter what you believe. If you will be honest with yourself you will be healed by applying these simple but painful truths to your life. Don't give up push through!

_____

_____

_____

_____

_____

_____

_____

_____

_____

_____

_____

_____

_____

_____

_____

_____

_____

_____

_____

Chapter 3

Fake It Till You Make It

By Debra Ann Sutterfield

Phillipians 4:13 KJ Version
I can do all things through Christ which strengtheneth me.

To find joy in your life you must first know that you are a precious jewel, beautiful in every way. To find victory and true joy, to be able to truly love anyone you must first love yourself.

For years I walked on a path where I was beat down I felt unloved. I have been lied to I was told I was ugly I was told I was worthless I was no good.

After a while I began to believe those words I mean, the person who was telling me this was supposed to be in love with me. Surely he wouldn't lie to me after all, I was the woman he chose to marry. I was the woman he chose to spend his life with. He must've truly believed those things if he was saying them to me. He said hurtful things, things that I will never forget they are embedded in my heart.

I spent 21 years married crying every day of my life. When I had children I thought it would make everything okay. I thought I would finally have someone to love me in return. I love them so very much but there was something bad wrong. I could not even love me. How can you teach children to love when you've never known what love truly was.

I read a book which talked about love tanks and how a mom and a dad when they have a baby are supposed to fill that baby's love tank but if one person is not sharing love and the other one is trying to love through their child instead of filling the baby's love tank it actually sucks the love right out of that baby. Looking back I realize that is what had happened to me when I was a child and now I was teaching it to my children.

Having this knowledge it left me with only one thing to do I had to learn to change who I was so that my children could grow and love. So they could become normal functioning human beings not broken and in bondage as my heart was. I had to break the bondage of my heart. The lies that kept me bound had to be set free.

But while you are reading this, you must know, I was not aware these were lies. I was in full belief that these were facts.

This is where my journey began and how I believe you can change your journey into the path of victory.

Matthew 8:13
"and as thou hast believed, so be it done unto thee."

Mathew 8:13 says
"What, you believe is what you become".

You see, I believed those words I heard, crying about them every day I did become lazy I was unloved I was unlovable! I no longer loved myself.

Proverbs 23:7
For as he thinketh in his heart, so is he:

When you believe something you begin to think about it in your heart you begin to change who you are. The words I thought about in my heart is who I became.

What you believe about you, becomes a reality! The value you believe you hold, is the value you become. What is your value? How do you value yourself? Who is the person you have created in your heart?

Please take a moment and write down who you are. Who do <u>you</u> feel you are? What is the true value you place in your own life? What is your self-worth? Please be honest about it. In order to grow you have to be honest with yourself and honorable to yourself. After this course is over you can come back to this page to evaluate your growth.

_____
_____
_____
_____
_____
_____
_____
_____
_____
_____
_____
_____
_____
_____
_____
_____
_____

The title of this chapter is "Fake It Till You Make It", and here is why. If we believe in our heart negative things about ourselves, if we believe lies we have been told or have told ourselves we have to retrain our beliefs. In the beginning of this journey retraining our beliefs will be the single most difficult thing we do.

You ask "why will it be difficult?" Because we are sold out in full commitment to the lies we believe about us.

So, what we are going to do is to create new words to describe us. Though these new words are true as God sees us, they will sound like lies and foreign words to us. We will recognize these words in other people but possibly not in ourselves.

We have to change the way we think. We have to change the words we use. And, we have to take out the trash.

Our main goal in this section is to begin the process of taking back what Satan has stolen from us. We may not feel that victory yet, but we are going to fake it till we make it!

We cannot live in victory and have a positive outlook if we keep garbage and negative words in our life. Let's take out the trash. Now, are you ready to begin your journey to victory?

Step 1: Think good thoughts.

Proverbs 23:7
"For as he thinketh in his heart, so is he:"

You may be like me. I had no idea how to think good thoughts.

Here is how I began. I got a dry erase marker and began with one thought which I wrote on my bathroom mirror so I could see it first thing in the morning and last thing at night before bed. I wrote boldly "YOU ARE BEAUTIFUL."

Those words felt good. I brushed my teeth looked at those words and smiled. I went to bed got up the next morning looked at those words and rubbed them off in anger. What was I thinking I'm not beautiful. Then remembering the promise I made to myself I angrily scribbled it back on the mirror and added "you are the daughter of the most high God!"

I came home that night brushed my teeth looked in the mirror scrubbed it clean. What was I doing trying to convince myself I had value to anyone especially God. Once again in anger I scrolled it even bigger and angrier onto my mirror. This scenario I played out day after day. I finally, after doing this over and over very calmly wrote it in a neat and legible fashion.

Something was beginning to happen to me. I was beginning to feel different. But could God love me? Yes, I am his child but look at all I have done against him. Could he love me? I thought of my own children. I thought how even when they did things to disappoint me, I still loved them enough to lay down my life for them. Wait.... God did that for me! "I Am The Daughter Of The Most High God!"

This is not an easy journey. I promise you this, this is a journey of victory. If you will follow these steps and get back on the path when you stumble, your life will change. You may be like me, not able to see that vision. Please make a promise to yourself that you will not give up. Victory is waiting.

Now let's begin. Here are a few words to begin. Please keep in mind you must start small. We are tearing down years of strong holds on our lives. We are taking baby steps to grow. Feel free to use some of my suggestions or think of some of your own.

Your homework for the week is to write the words down. Read them several times a day. Say them with authority out loud. Find two people here in your group today to be your accountability partners. Exchange phone numbers and speak with each daily stating your positive words you have chosen And allowing your partners time to state theirs. One suggestion is to choose the words you want to believe about yourself.

❧ I am beautiful!
❧ I am the daughter of the most high God!
❧ I am drug free!
❧ I am happy!
❧ I am successful!
❧ I am a great wife!
❧ I am an awesome mom!
❧ I am wonderfully made!
❧ I am _____!

This is your journey! Beginning today write it the way it should be. It won't be easy. It won't always go our way, but we have the ability to change who we believe ourselves to be.

Philippians 4:13
I can do all things through Christ which strengtheneth me.

Daily Practice

I am the daughter of the Most High God, The One True God, The Great I Am. His Holy Spirit, Power, Life and Wisdom is within me. It surrounds me and moves through me. The Holy Spirit is pure and good and His Power is realized through the action of my words and behavior.

His Spirit is perfect in goodness. Because His Spirit lives in me, only goodness goes out of me, and only goodness will return to me. In me allowing Him to, he will govern me leading me into right actions.

The Spirit of God establishes peace, joy and calmness in all personal, family and business life, establishing peace in all relationships. I am happy, calm and content in my life. Everything that I think, say or do is inspired through God in love and divine wisdom.

He leads me to do right and make right decisions. Those decisions lead me to love others, to forgive others, and to grow in God's perfect will. These actions allow me to forgive myself for offenses against others and against myself. His divine wisdom has made it clear to me that I am not responsible for others' offenses against me.

I am filled with enthusiasm, joy, energy and inspiration. I am surrounded by the love of friends and family. I am in constant recognition of God's presence and all of his blessings.

I represent that "Tree Of Life," which sacrificed and paid the price for my sins. I accept his payment for my forgiveness. His sacrifice gives me the power over darkness and evil, the power and wisdom that never sleeps, but gives life.

As a result of realizing that His Spirit lives in me, happiness, health and prosperity will immediately manifest itself and become evident in my life, knowing all I receive is a blessing and a promise from God.

I am constantly aware of his Divine Presence in my life, the happiness that comes with it and my increasing blessings. I am aware and ready when he brings someone into my life for the purpose of sharing his love.

I believe these words to be true and evident. I know it is the very presence of God and His Holy Spirit living in me, moving me into righteousness and healing. Because of his Spiritual Presence I feel peace, joy, and an abundance of blessings. I feel more energized because He is the God that never tires, never sleeps, and sustains our every need.

I expect miracles and greater goodness because He lives in me. I again affirm that this is the very presence of God and His Holy Spirit living in me, creating in me what is new, good and true, establishing in me a beauty that all can see.

I accept that His promises are true. I know and believe these words are the evidence of His truth. I Am The Daughter Of The Great I Am!

I AM

1. A child of God (Romans 8:16)

2. Redeemed from the hand of the enemy (Psalms 107:2)

3. Forgiven (Colossians 1:13-14)

4. Saved by Grace through Faith (Ephesians 2:8)

5. Justified (Romans 5:1)

6. Sanctified (I Corinthians 6:11)

7. A new creature (II Corinthians 5:17)

8. Partaker of HIS divine nature (II Peter 1:4)

9. Redeemed from the curse of the law (Galatians 3:13)

10. Delivered from the powers of darkness (Colossians 1:13)

11. Led by the Spirit of God (Romans 8:14)

12. A son/daughter of God (Romans 8:14)

13. Kept in safety wherever I go (Psalms 91:11)

14. Getting all my needs met by Christ Jesus (Philippians 4:19)

15. Casting all my cares on Christ Jesus (I Peter 5:7)

16. Strong in the Lord and in the Power of His might (Ephesians 6:10)

17. Doing all things through Christ who strengthens

me (Philippians 4:13)

18. An heir of God and joint heirs with Christ Jesus (Romans 8:17)

19. Heir to the blessing of Abraham (Galatians 3:13-14)

20. Observing and obeying the Lord's commandments (Deuteronomy 28:12)

21. Blessed coming in and blessed going out (Deuteronomy 28:6)

22. An heir of eternal life (I John 5:11-12)

23. Blessed with all spiritual blessings (Ephesians 1:3)

24. Healed by His stripes (I Peter 2:24)

25. Exercising my authority over the enemy (Luke 10:19)

26. Above only and not beneath (Deuteronomy 28:13)

27. More than a conqueror (Romans 8:37)

28. Establishing God's Word here on earth (Matthew 16:19)

29. An over comer by the blood of the Lamb and the word of my testimony

(Revelation 12:11)

30. Daily overcoming the devil (I John 4:4)

31. Not moved by what I see (II Corinthians 4:18)

32. Walking by faith and not by sight (II Corinthians 5:7)

33. Casting down vain imaginations (II Corinthians 10:4-5)

34. Bringing every thought into captivity (II Corinthians 10:5)

35. Being transformed by renewing my mind (Romans 12:1-2)

36. A laborer together with God (I Corinthians 3:9)

37. The righteousness of God in Christ (II Corinthians 5:21)

38. An imitator of Jesus (Ephesians 5:1)

39. The Light of the World (Matthew 5:14)

40. Blessing the Lord at all times and continually praising the Lord with my mouth (Psalms 34:1)

<u>Notes</u>

On this page take the time to examine how you may
relate to the chapter you have just read. How will you
be able to utilize the points made in this chapter? How
will you apply them to your actions and your daily
decisions? In healing, it is so important to stop lying to
yourself. Be honest, this is between you and God.
Remember God loves you, no matter what you believe.
If you will be honest with yourself you will be healed
by applying these simple but painful truths to your life.
Don't give up push through!

Chapter 4

AS WE SPEAK

By Donna Story

[6] And the tongue is a fire, a world of iniquity: so is the tongue among our members, that it defileth the whole body, and setteth on fire the course of nature; and it is set on fire of hell. **James 3:6** King James Version (KJV)

Words - what do they mean to us? Do we flap our lips and move our tongue just to hear ourselves talk? Are we afraid of the silence? You know, God gave us two ears and just one mouth. Doesn't it make sense then that we should listen twice as much as we talk?

James 1:19 says we need to be swift to hear and slow to speak. Proverbs 10:19 says don't talk so much. You keep putting your foot in your mouth. Be sensible and turn off the flow! Proverbs 15:28 says a good man thinks before he speaks: the evil man pours out his evil words without a thought. Proverbs 17:27 & 28 says the man of a few words and a settled mind is wise; therefore, even a fool is thought to be wise when he is silent. It pays him to keep his mouth shut. Proverbs 18:21 says those who love to talk will suffer the consequences. Men have died for saying the wrong thing! Proverbs 21:11 & 23 says the wise man learns by listening; the simpleton can learn only by seeing scorners punish. Keep your mouth closed and you'll stay out of trouble.

Words - how do we use them? Do we use them to build up or to tear down? My mom would tell us girls, "if you have nothing good to say, say nothing at all." Proverbs 15:26 says the Lord hates the thoughts of the wicked, but delights in kind words.

Did you know that words can bring healing? Here are 8 words that can bring healing in any relationship: I WAS WRONG, WILL YOU PLEASE FORGIVE ME?

Here are a few scriptures you need to learn:

Psalm 34:12 & 13 – Do you want a long, good life? Then watch your tongue! Keep your lips from lying (maybe this is another topic we should touch on).

Proverbs 12:18 – Some people like to make cutting remarks, but the words of the wise soothe and heal.

Proverbs 15:4 – Gentle words cause life and health; griping brings discouragement.

Proverbs 16:24 – Kind words are like honey – enjoyable and healthful.

Words are so important in our lives. I was listening to a preacher on TV giving his testimony. He was talking about a problem he had that he never recognized. Until, one day, a friend stopped him in his tracks and told him how awful he had spoken to some friends of his. This preacher was a Christian, a pastor filled with the Holy Ghost. But, here he was, confronted with a problem he never admitted he had. His friend took him aside and said, "Man, God told me you have an abandonment issue. God says that, when you meet new people, you drive them away with your words before they can get close to you so you won't hurt when they choose to not be a friend or if they would, they might leave some day." You need to change your words. You need to speak love and not discouragement. You need to let God take care of your relationships. God used this friend to change his life. Our words, the vehicle, we use to drive people away from us is the same vehicle we use to draw people near to us.

I had been doing the same thing in my life. I was so tired of friends leaving my life I no longer encouraged anyone to want to be my friend. I stopped speaking to people. But, what was worse, I stopped listening also. If we want a friend, we not only need to speak truth and give good advice, sharing in each other's lives, we also need to be a good listener. We can't come to know another person if we don't listen. I like how James said that we need to be swift to hear and slow to speak. God had to show me that friends come and go as He wants. Some are for a time, some for a season, and some for a lifetime. I had to make God my lifetime friend so He could show me how to be a friend, and to cherish that friend for whatever length of time they were there for.   Our words should be like we are - precious jewels, words, a person can savor, and hold in their hearts to cherish. How will your friends remember you? There are two women in my church that I admire. They always speak such kind words to everyone. The children in my church love these ladies, because they know they will always hear good things spoken over them. I have used them as an example in my own life, speaking good words to those I talk to. That's showing God's love to one another.

Talking about friends, how do we treat those we supposedly love the most? Do you speak words of love? If you have a spouse, the words you speak over him will be the kind of spouse you will have. Let this sink in for a moment. I want to use this as an example: have you ever gone forward to ask for prayer for a healing? Do you feel God move on you and you testify that you have been healed? Then the next day you run into someone at the store and they ask how you are, and you tell them all about your aches and pains and how bad you have been feeling. Tell me, what happened to the healing God gave you? God is not a gift snatcher. Once He gives us something, He doesn't take it away from us. We decide in our own minds what to do with that healing. Do we except it one minute and then next throw it away? We can't have two conflicting reports. Whose report are we going to believe? If you want to keep the report of the Lord, then you have to speak it as such even if your body isn't accepting it at the time. We keep speaking God's Word until our body lines up with it. So, if you want a spouse that treats you well and is loving, then that is what you need to be speaking over him and about him. You cannot run to your friends and say rotten things about him and expect God to give you the good. The bad you say erases the good you want. Talk everything over just between you and God and let Him tell you what you say to others.

Nothing makes me madder than to hear a parent say bad things to their child or about their child. Why would anyone try to act any other way than how they hear people talk about them? Our words matter! They bring life or death, sickness or healing, encouragement or destruction, joy or sadness. What do you want your words to do?

God had to deal with me about the words I was speaking, not only over someone, but to someone. We hurt those we love the most when we get angry or upset about something, and it doesn't even have to be their fault. But, we assume they should understand and have broad shoulders, and we usually end up fighting because we say things out of anger that should never be spoken. God told me to stop doing that because it just drove that person away. He told me to get in my prayer closet before I ever talked to someone and tell it all to Him. God knows our hearts and our hurts and frustrations. He can handle us telling Him all of it. God finally helped me to see how I was hurting others with my words and, by telling Him, He helped me get rid of the bad before I would speak it. It's nice to know I don't always have to speak or I can choose to say nice words. God helped me to change my outlook and how I thought. Did you know that what we think is what comes out of our mouths? <u>Romans 12:2</u> – says, and do not be conformed to this world, but be transformed by the renewing of your mind, that you may prove what is that good and acceptable and perfect will of God (so we think, so we are).

God's perfect will is love. It's about us learning about His love toward us who are His creation. It's about our love to Him that we show to others. We can't love as the world loves because it comes from the flesh. But we love with God's love by letting our minds be renewed daily with God's Word.

From the front cover to the back cover the Bible is God's love story to us. We can't come to fully understand that unless we read His Word daily and think upon it always. When we are in any situation we should let what God's Word has put in our minds guide us. What we think, therefore, we speak. Are we going to let healing and love, come from our mouths, or destruction?

Here I want to encourage you to read the first 3 chapters of James. I'm going to give you some scriptures to highlight that speak on this topic: James 1:5, 18-23, 26 – James 3:2-10.

I hope you will start praying and speaking God's Word over your own life and over your loved ones. Only God's Word should be used. From now on, do not speak blessings in one breath and cursing's in the next. I know we are all guilty of this to some extent. What we believe in our hearts and speak with our mouth is who and what we are. Let's have God's love proceed from us.

I just saw the title of a TV program that said, "Mind over Matter, Heal Yourself." We need to be careful of what we watch, read and listen to. What I'm talking about isn't a name it and claim it thing, or a mind over matter. It's about believing the Word of God and applying it to our lives. If we want to speak God's truth over our lives, it's important for us to read the Bible and ask God to give us understanding. God is not some magic show, but He is the truth and the light. Magic disappears but God's Word endures forever.

I encourage you to look up scriptures on lying and see what God's Word tells us about these words that come from our mouths. May God bless us all and give us understanding of His Word and wisdom to apply it to our lives.

As We Speak Assignment

What does your mind dwell on? Do you let good things sink into your mind? What do you read? What do you watch on TV? What kind of music do you listen to? All of these avenues affect what is put into your mind and what eventually comes out of your mouth and also how we act.

If we put nothing but trash into our mind only trash will come out. We need to put this scripture into our hearts and get this mind set:
Philippians 4:8
King James Version (KJV)
8 Finally, brethren, whatsoever things are true, whatsoever things are honest, whatsoever things are just, whatsoever things are pure, whatsoever things are lovely, whatsoever things are of good report; if there be any virtue, and if there be any praise, think on these things.

Make a list of the material you allow to enter your mind.

_____
_____
_____
_____
_____
_____
_____
_____
_____
_____

Read over the list and then note any changes that should be made according to God's word.

_____

_____

_____

_____

_____

_____

_____

_____

_____

_____

Have these views affected how you think about the choices you have made in the media you consume and the company you keep? Has it changed the value of the words you will choose to speak?

_____

_____

_____

_____

_____

_____

_____

_____

_____

_____

_____

_____

_____

_____

_____

_____

_____

_____

_____

_____

Notes

On this page take the time to examine how you may relate to the chapter you have just read. How will you be able to utilize the points made in this chapter? How will you apply them to your actions and your daily decisions? In healing, it is so important to stop lying to yourself. Be honest, this is between you and God. Remember God loves you, no matter what you believe. If you will be honest with yourself you will be healed by applying these simple but painful truths to your life. Don't give up push through!

_____

_____

_____

_____

_____

_____

_____

_____

_____

_____

_____

_____

_____

_____

_____

_____

_____

_____

_____

_____

_____

_____

_____

Chapter 5

Taking a Stand on God's Word

By Debra Ann Sutterfield

[12] For *the word of God is quick, and powerful*, and sharper than any twoedged sword, piercing even to the dividing asunder of soul and spirit, and of the joints and marrow, and is a discerner of the thoughts and intents of the heart. **Hebrews 4:12** King James Version (KJV)

This week I was diagnosed with an ascending aortic aneurysm. After days of worrying over the consequences about the fatality if it were to rupture, I came to one strong conclusion. I am teaching others to stand in faith and stand on God's word. If I do not stand on the same faith I am preaching to others, where do I truly stand in God's eyes? Whose report shall I believe?

God gave me symptoms most people are not fortunate enough to have. We never would have known about this aneurysm without those symptoms. This would most certainly have been fatal and only detected after death. As I have worried and fretted, where was my faith? Where was the faith that I insist you stand? Today, I take a stand! I choose to believe God's report! I **will** believe God's report!

Psalms 103: 1-5
Bless the LORD, O my soul: and all that is within me, bless his holy name. Bless the LORD, O my soul, and forget not all his benefits: Who forgiveth all thine iniquities; <u>who healeth all thy diseases;</u> Who redeemeth thy life from destruction; who crowneth thee with loving kindness and tender mercies; Who satisfieth thy mouth with good things; so that thy youth is renewed like the eagle's.

If God heals diseases, I will stand on that word. That promise is good enough for me. Jesus tells me that Satan wants me dead. He says in John 10:10 *The thief does not come except to* **steal,** *and to* **kill** *and to* **destroy.** *I have come that you may have life, and have it more abundantly.*

58

I will cast down **my** thoughts and **my** imaginations that do not line up with the word that I base my life on, the word that has called me to preach, the word, that shall til death, be my testimony.

Second Corinthians 10:4,5 KJV
[4] (For the weapons of our warfare are not carnal, but mighty through God to the pulling down of strong holds;) [5] <u>Casting down imaginations, and every high thing that exalteth itself against the knowledge of God,</u> and bringing into captivity every thought to the obedience of Christ,

I will guard my lips and watch my words so that what I say is aligned with what God says. It is to easy to let our negative words that do not agree with God and his promises slip out of our mouth.

Psalms 141:3
Set a watch, O LORD, before my mouth; keep the door of my lips.

Psalms 17:3
Thou hast proved mine heart; thou hast visited me in the night; thou hast tried me, and shalt find nothing; I am purposed that my mouth shall not transgress.

We must watch and guard carefully the words we use. A negative word spoken becomes a weapon of attack for the enemy. Any words of fear or doubt will be used like a snare and a prison. This is why it is so important and the reason we have mentioned repeatedly how we should speak to ourselves and about ourselves.

Proverbs *6:2*
Thou art snared with the words of thy mouth, thou art taken with the words of thy mouth.

Don't give Satan any power or authority that he has no right to have. It is important that we exercise our authority over him at all times. If I am to teach you to stand in faith, I am now brought to you as an example of that same faith. I shall now lead by that example, going past fear, but taking authority over evil and pleading the blood of Jesus over myself with that authority. You have that same authority no matter what you are going through. If it is your health, an addiction, a broken heart, your past, or abuse. It does not matter because we have authority to claim victory over our problem, over any problem. God loves us and has given us authority if we choose to use it.

Mark 16:17,18
To them that believe in Jesus, they have authority and power to perform miracles.

Mark 16:17-18 KJV
[17] And <u>these signs shall follow them that believe;</u> <u>In my name shall</u> they cast out devils; they shall speak with new tongues; [18] They shall take up serpents; and if they drink any deadly thing, it shall not hurt them; <u>they shall lay hands on the</u> <u>sick, and they shall recover.</u>

Do you believe in Jesus? Have you ever acted in authority in his name, knowing what you state must be obeyed?

Mark 16:20
And they went forth, and preached everywhere, the Lord working with them, and confirming the word with signs following. Amen.

I believe in every word! I claim victory through that word! I challenge you to stand in faith on the infallible word of God. When you have done all you can, stand and know God is!

My pastor's wife once said "you can doubt in your mind, but know the truth in your heart. The devil leads us to doubt in our mind as he plants his deceitful thoughts, but in our heart we must know God has given us victory. We may not see the victory just yet, but we must keep claiming that victory." The devil has told me I am going to die. But, God has told me, "I know the plans I have for you." Who should I believe? **God was, is, and will be forever more, a never-changing God**. Satan's future is an eternal bondage to hell, a very real hell. Who's word should I believe? I choose this day to stand on God's promise. He knows the plans he has for me.

Jeremiah 29:11 tells us he has plans for us. I like the NIV translation for this.

Jeremiah 29:11
"For I know the plans I have for you" declares

The Lord, "plans to prosper you and not to harm you, plans to give you hope and a future."

Stand on faith. Faith is knowing it will happen, with no earthly clue, how it will happen.

Hebrews 11:1
Now faith is the substance of things hoped for, the evidence of things not seen.
Probably the most difficult thing to do is to stand on faith, but, without it, we can't believe that Jesus died for our sins, for our salvation, or that we may live eternally with him. Faith is the power of victory! The final thought begins in your mind! As a man, thinketh so is he!

Singapore has more medical technology than any location in Asia. You can have any medical test you choose. People who can afford it flock to Singapore for medical tests. Would it surprise you to know that there are more diseases in Singapore than anywhere in Asia? The United States of America is the sickest and most diseased country on the planet! If you pull into any parking lot, the first eight spaces in each row are dedicated to handicapped people. Those numbers are attributed to a smaller parking lot, the bigger the lot the more the spaces. Why? We quickly flock to the doctor and we not only receive the report the doctor gives us, but we eagerly believe it. The first thing we do is start talking about it, and tell everyone who will listen.

At a recent prayer service we prayed for many people to be healed. Now hear me when I say this, our words speak our faith, or our lack thereof. After praying for one woman who came down wanting a healing, she threw her hands in the air saying, "I have a praise report." We all turned, excited to hear her claim her healing as she said, "I got a letter from the government they are going to pay for my medications." When you look at this example, you have to know, why should God heal her, she has just announced the government is taking care of her so she doesn't really need God. We are all guilty of claiming and believing the bad report. We receive it like it's a gift. We claim the negative words we have been told or we have felt, we hold on to them like they are an old friend. Our entire life we have spent believing the garbage until it made us who we are. Why? Because the final thought begins in our mind!

Romans 10:9
That if thou shalt confess with thy mouth the Lord Jesus, and shalt believe in thine heart that God hath raised him from the dead, thou shalt be saved.

To be saved, we must believe and speak the facts. Fact One: speak out of your mouth The Lord Jesus. Fact Two: believe that God raised Jesus from the grave. We cannot speak of faith in another God, a horoscope or self. We can only speak of God, Jesus and the Holy Spirit in salvation. The final thought has to start in your mind and be completed with your words.

We know God heals us if we ask him, but we have to be obedient and stand on the rock in faith. We cannot slip up and talk about things as we see them, as the doctor has said or how someone has made us feel, maybe names we have been called. We must speak the healing. We must call the things as we want them to be, the things that we have asked God to change in us, as if they already are. I am the healed. I have overcome. I am victorious! Why, do I say these things? Because, I have learned them from the master.

Romans 4:17
even God, who quickeneth the dead, and calleth those things which be not as though they were.

We must claim the words. We must claim the victory! We must claim healing! It does not matter what we feel, we must call those things that are not as if they are.

Proverbs 18:21
Death and life are in the power of the tongue: and they that love it shall eat the fruit thereof.

The power of life and death are in the tongue! Choose life! Choose victory! Eat the fruits of your positive words. Using negative words or dying words is to choose death. Choose life!

All of this being said, if this claim of authority over our lives is important, why should we not incorporate it into every part of our life? In the Old Testament, we read of fathers speaking blessings over their children before they die. I say, we should speak blessings over our children, our spouse, job, home etc. every day. Think of the impact you would have by taking authority and speaking blessings and health over every aspect of your life. The words you speak can be a blessing or a curse. The words you speak over your children, your spouse, your friend, or yourself, will become evident in the outcome of the blessings. You say they are just words, but words become a reality. It appears saying positive affirmations over those you love would be a simple task to accomplish. Changing a lifetime of habits is not an easy task. You must diligently apply this technique until it is mastered. Every thought must be taken by authority. Because, when you have the thought and speak the words, it becomes concrete.

2nd Corinthians 10:5
Casting down imaginations, and every high thing that exalteth itself against the knowledge of God, and bringing into captivity every thought to the obedience of Christ;

It is a necessity, if you want victory, to cast down your imagination. God is perfect in all ways and yet we pit our words against His knowledge. One of the acronyms we like to use is ANT. Exterminate all ANTs: **A**ny **N**egative **T**houghts.

Be obedient to God. Stand on his promises. Cast down your imagination and anything that goes against what his word says or becomes bigger than or more important than Him. Make your words obedient to the word of God. Just think of the power your words have. Thinking of the authority God has given you. How have we used words to place our self in bondage? That, alone, is mind boggling. We are living in the prison that all along we have had the keys to open the door and walk out. With the knowledge you now have, ponder how you can change your life, your children, husband, or friend. God has given us the authority, but somewhere along the course, we never realized we had it.

God wants the best for his children. He has given us so many promises, but we think they are for others but not for us. The Holy Bible says that God is no respecter of persons. That simply means that his word is for any of his children that believe in him. Remember, we must believe in our heart and confess with our mouth The Lord Jesus, and we shall be saved. For, with the heart, man believes unto righteousness, but, with the mouth, confession is made unto salvation. Our words lead us to salvation. Our words lead us to condemnation. Our words can keep us in bondage of our past or our words can set us free to live a new life.

What words will you choose?

Who will you bless today?

What words have kept you in bondage?

What words will you choose for victory?

How will you use words to bless others?

Who will you speak blessings over?

What areas of their lives do you want to see changed?

What areas of your own life will you speak blessings over?

Don't you think it is time to take a stand on God's word and utilize the authority He has given you?

_____
_____
_____
_____
_____
_____
_____
_____
_____
_____
_____

SATAN'S WEAPONS

The enemy (Satan) uses our past and/or current generations to hinder our Heavenly Father's destiny for our life. Satan uses the weapons listed below to separate us from our Heavenly Father. These weapons separate us from ourselves so that we can't love ourselves, and separates us from others.

ABANDONED	ANGER	ANXIETY
ARGUMENTAT	BETRAYAL	BITTERNESS
BLAME	CONDEMNED	CONFUSION
CONTROL	CRITICAL	DECEIVED
DEFILEMENT	DESERTED	DOWN
DOUBTFUL	DISCOURAGEMENT	
EMPTY	ENVIOUS	FEAR
FRUSTRATED	GLOOMY	GUILTY
GRIEF-STRICKEN	GREEDY	HURT
HARDHEARTED	HATEFULNESS	JEALOUS
HOPELESSNESS	HUMILIATED	MEAN
INADEQUATE	INSIGNIFICANT	INSULTED
INTIMIDATED	JUDGMENTAL	LONELINESS
NEGATIVE	MISERABLE	OFFENDED
NERVOUS	STUBBORN	VAIN
POWERLESS	REBELLIOUS	REJECTION

SELF-CENTERED	SHAME	STRESSED
THREATENED	TIMID	TENSE
UNFORGIVENESS	USELESS	WORTHLESS
WORRIED	IRRITATED	

Our Heavenly Father's gift to us is <u>LOVE</u>, which contains the blessings of joy, peace, longsuffering, gentleness, goodness, faith, meekness, temperance.

GALATIANS 5:22-23

God is love and promises and His love will never fail!

Notes

On this page take the time to examine how you may relate to the chapter you have just read. How will you be able to utilize the points made in this chapter? How will you apply them to your actions and your daily decisions? In healing, it is so important to stop lying to yourself. Be honest, this is between you and God. Remember God loves you, no matter what you believe. If you will be honest with yourself you will be healed by applying these simple but painful truths to your life. Don't give up push through!

_____

_____

_____

_____

_____

_____

_____

_____

_____

_____

_____

_____

_____

_____

_____

_____

_____

_____

_____

_____

_____

_____

_____

_____

Chapter 6

Before You Can Heal....
You Have To Love
Yourself!

by Debra Ann Sutterfield

[39] And the second is like unto it, Thou shalt love thy neighbour **as thyself**.

Matthew 22:39 King James Version (KJV)

Maybe, one of the hardest things to do is to learn to love yourself. We grow up hearing negative things said to us and we begin to claim ownership of those words. We begin to believe that is who we are. Between words and life experiences loving our self doesn't seem something we deserve. As a child I can remember feeling shame. My dad was the neighborhood drunk, it was no secret. Drunken parties, brawls and arrests were a regular part of my childhood. The night my brother was born my dad was in jail. I felt shame and embarrassment.

My mom took us to church every Sunday morning, Sunday night, and Wednesday night. I can remember walking in church, mom would tell us to stand straight and hold our heads up no one else knew what we were going through. As we would walk down the aisle I could hear the good church ladies say, "there goes Gail and those pitiful little children." Shame and embarrassment.

At sixteen, I married. I know, you are saying, "wow," but I needed an escape, and I was in love. There was a problem with that statement. I didn't know how to love; he didn't know how to love. There you have it, two broken people trying to do something neither had been taught to do. The good church ladies said I was pregnant. That hurt (in those days you didn't have a baby outside of marriage). I quit going to church, I was hurt. I read my Bible at home and prayed, something was wrong that I just didn't get. Years went by, and my husband called me names and embarrassed me any opportunity he had. I cried every day, and I believed the things I was being called, they hurt. More shame and embarrassment.

I eventually started going to church again, but it didn't fix me. I thought I wasn't close enough to God, so I took every study course the church offered. The courses didn't fix me either. I was not realizing that the problem was, I was not striving to get closer to God. My problem was learning to love me and allowing God to get close to me.

YOU WILL NEVER BE ABLE TO LOVE THE HEAVENLY FATHER OR YOUR NEIGHBOR AS YOU DESIRE UNTIL YOU FIRST LOVE YOURSELF.

Why do I tell you these things? Not because I still live in it or believe it any longer, but to let you know, I didn't love me. I actually had no reason to love me, who would? I tell you these things because many of us have the problem of not being able to love ourselves. If my story can help you tear down the strongholds that keep you from loving yourself and giving you victory in your life, then I am willing to bear it for you. As I have found peace through learning to love myself, I feel these words can lead you to freedom also.

Without being able to love yourself many things can happen. You can develop an array of emotional problems as well as health issues.

LOVING ONE'S SELF IS A GREAT STEP OUT OF ALL SELF-HATRED DISEASES.

Matthew 22: 36-40
Master, which is the great commandment in the law? Jesus said unto him, Thou shalt love the Lord

thy God with all thy heart, and with all thy soul, and with all thy mind. This is the first and great commandment. And the second is like unto it, Thou shalt love thy neighbour as thyself. On these two commandments hang all the law and the prophets.

COMMANDMENT ONE:
THOU SHALT LOVE THE LORD THY GOD WITH ALL THY HEART, AND WITH ALL THY SOUL, AND WITH ALL THY MIND.

COMMANDMENT TWO:
THOU SHALT LOVE THY NEIGHBOUR AS THYSELF.

COMMANDMENT THREE:
THOU SHALT LOVE THYSELF MAKING IT POSSIBLE TO LOVE YOUR GOD AND YOUR NEIGHBOUR AS YOUR HEAVENLY FATHER COMMANDED.

I had read these scriptures and had them memorized, but I had missed one vital part. "Love thy neighbor as thyself".

I got that love thy neighbor part but "*as thyself*" never got through to me. I didn't like me at all and, love? Well, how can you love if you don't know how to love something so unworthy, so unlovable?

THE STRATEGY OF SATAN HASN'T
CHANGED. IT IS TO GET YOU TO BELIEVE
THE LIE THAT YOU ARE INSECURE,
UNWORTHY, AND INFERIOR,
AND TO WALK IN REBELLION AND
REJECTION.

We cannot allow Satan to have control of our lives. We must take back the life he has stolen from us. In order to do this, we must first recognize the lies he has convinced us to believe.

You see, you are worthy. Nothing you have ever done can separate you from Christ. He loves us and forgives us when we ask for that forgiveness and ask him into our lives. We have to turn from our sins and turn to him but he finds us worthy, beautiful and his precious child. How could we be less than how he sees us. How could we be anything less than what God has said we are?

Satan lies and steals from us. He tries to keep us in our past and shackled to the lies. When we ask God for forgiveness, an odd thing happens. First, we feel relief, like a huge burden has been lifted from us; then, we start hearing a small voice from inside us telling us "you know you aren't really forgiven, don't you?" That small voice starts pecking away at us until it tears us down. We begin to feel more down and depressed than before we asked for forgiveness. That small voice is Satan. He does not want us to have freedom from our burdens. He wants to keep us beat down and under his control.

1 Peter 5:8
Be sober, be vigilant; because your adversary the devil, as a roaring lion, walketh about, seeking whom he may devour.

We have the power of victory if we choose to use it, by applying a few simple rules to our life. This may be painful but worth the effort.

We need to be careful of the words we use to describe ourselves. But we also need to use words to encourage ourselves daily. If we have allowed others' words to tear us down, we need to now use words to undo that damage. We need to find value in ourselves and declare it out loud. We need to say these words with authority. Take charge of your life, stand strong, and claim your victory!

There is a battle of 2 wolves inside all of us. One is evil - it is anger, jealousy, greed, resentment, lies, inferiority, and ego. The other is good - it is joy, peace, love, hope, humility, kindness, empathy and truth. The wolf that wins is the one we feed.

You cannot have a positive life and a negative mind at the same time. That being said we must change what we think and say about ourselves. If you have good and positive thoughts and words, you will produce a positive outlook making the fruit of your life good. If you have negative thoughts and words, it will produce a negative outlook and the fruit of your life will not grow richly, but will be bad. When you nurture bad, bad grows. When you nurture good, good grows.

Today decide to take back what the devil has stolen from you. Just begin and move even if it is one inch at a time. One inch puts you one inch closer than you were before you began.

Ever since Eve, women have been believing Satan's lies and so have their daughters. When you are able to tear down the strongholds Satan has over you, life will begin to change in a positive way. It does not mean life will always be sunshine, but it does mean you will hold the keys to get out of Satan's control a whole lot faster and stay out a whole lot longer.

Proverbs 23:7 "For as he thinketh in his heart, so is he."

Remember, change the way you think change the words you use. I was so negative for so many years I had no idea that it was the negativity that kept me in depression. I thought negatively and spoke negatively. When I began trying to say nice things to me (things that felt like lies by the way), I slowly began to come out of my depression.

1 Peter 4:8
And above all things have fervent love among yourselves: for love shall cover the multitude of sins.

Changing my words changed my attitude. Changing your words can change your attitude, too.

40 HEALING SCRIPTURES
Standing on these words can be healing for your soul as well as your body. Read them over and over.

Romans 10 tells us that faith comes from hearing and hearing from the Word of Christ. To help us believe God for healing ourselves, our friends and our families it helps to have a good understanding of the Scriptures concerning healing. These Scriptures are small enough to be written on a business card sized bit of paper, carried around and memorized. All these are taken from the New King James Version of the Bible.

1] Exodus 15:26 said, **"If you diligently heed the voice of the Lord your God and do what is right in His sight, give ear to His commandments and keep all His statutes, I will put none of the diseases on you which I have brought on the Egyptians. For I am the Lord who heals you."**

2] Exodus 23:25 **"So you shall serve the LORD your God, and He will bless your bread and your water. And I will take sickness away from the midst of you."**

3] II Chronicles 7:14 **"If My people who are called by My name will humble themselves, and pray and seek My face, and turn from their wicked ways, then I will hear from heaven, and will forgive their sin and heal their land."**

4] Psalm 30:2 **"O Lord my God, I cried out to You,**

and You healed me."

5] Psalm 6:2 "Have mercy on me. O Lord, for I am weak; O Lord, heal me, for my bones are troubled."

6] Psalm 103:1-4 "Bless the Lord, O my soul; And all that is within me, bless His Holy Name! (2)Bless the Lord, O my soul, And forget not all His benefits: (3)Who forgives all your iniquities, Who heals all your diseases, (4)Who redeems your life from destruction, Who crowns you with loving kindness and tender mercies."

7] Psalm 107:20 "He sent His Word and healed them, and delivered them from their destructions."

8] Psalm 147:3 "He heals the brokenhearted and binds up their wounds."

9] Proverbs 3:7-8 "Do not be wise in your own eyes; Fear the Lord and depart from evil. (8)It will be health to your flesh, and strength to your bones."

10] Proverbs 4:20-22 "My son, give attention to my words; Incline your ear to my sayings. (21)Do not let them depart from your eyes; Keep them in the midst of your heart; (22)For they are life to those who find them, and health to all their flesh."

11] Isaiah 53:5 "But He was wounded for our transgressions, He was bruised for our iniquities; The chastisement for our peace was upon Him, and by His stripes we are healed."

12] <u>Isaiah 58:8</u> "Then your light shall break forth like the morning, your healing shall spring forth speedily, and your righteousness shall go before you; The glory of the Lord shall be your guard."

13] <u>Isaiah 61:1</u> "The Spirit of the Lord God is upon Me, because the Lord has anointed Me to preach good tidings to the poor; He has sent Me to heal the brokenhearted, to proclaim liberty to the captives, and the opening of the prison to those who are bound;"

14] <u>Deuteronomy 30:19-20</u> "I call heaven and earth as witnesses today against you, *that* I have set before you life and death, blessing and cursing; therefore choose life, that both you and your descendants may live; that you may love the LORD your God, that you may obey His voice, and that you may cling to Him, for He *is* your life and the length of your days; and that you may dwell in the land which the LORD swore to your fathers, to Abraham, Isaac, and Jacob, to give them."

15] <u>Jeremiah 17:14</u> "Heal me, O Lord, and I shall be healed; Save me, and I shall be saved, for You are my praise."

16] <u>Jeremiah 30:17</u> "For I will restore health to you and heal you of your wounds, "says the Lord, 'Because they called you an outcast saying: 'This is Zion; No one seeks her.'"

17] Jeremiah 33:6 "Behold, I will bring it health and healing; I will heal them and reveal to them the abundance of peace and truth."

18] Hosea 6:1 "Come, and let us return to the Lord; For He has torn, but He will heal us; He has stricken, but He will bind us up."

19] John 9:31 "Now we know that God does not hear sinners; but if anyone is a worshiper of God and does His will, He hears him."

20] Malachi 4:2 "But to you who fear My name, the Sun of Righteousness shall arise with healing in His wings; And you shall go and grow fat like stall-fed calves."

21] Matthew 4:23 "And Jesus went about all Galilee, teaching in their synagogues, preaching the gospel of the kingdom, and healing all kinds of sickness and all kinds of disease among the people."

22] Matthew 8:13 "Then Jesus said to the centurion, "Go your way; And as you have believed, so let it be done for you." And his servant was healed that same hour."

23] Matthew 8:16 "When evening had come, they brought to Him many who were demon-possessed. And He cast out the spirits with a word, and healed all who were sick."

24] Matthew 9:35 "Then Jesus went about all the cities and villages, teaching in their synagogues, preaching the gospel of the kingdom, and healing every sickness and every disease among the people."

25] Matthew 10:1 "And when He had called His twelve disciples to Him, He gave them power over unclean spirits, to cast them out, and to heal all kinds of sickness and all kinds of disease."

26] Matthew 10:8 "Heal the sick, cleanse the lepers, raise the dead, cast out demons. Freely you have received, freely give."

27] Matthew 12:22 "Then one was brought to Him who was demon-possessed, blind and mute; And He healed him, so that the blind and mute man both spoke and saw."

28] Matthew 14:14 "And when Jesus went out He saw a great multitude; and He was moved with compassion for them, and healed their sick."

29] Luke 6:19 "And the whole multitude sought to touch Him, for power went out from Him and healed them all."

30] Luke 9:6 "So they departed and went through the towns, preaching the gospel and healing everywhere." (The twelve are sent out)

31] Luke 10:8-9 "Whatever city you enter, and they

receive you, eat such things as are set before you. (9)And heal the sick there, and say to them, 'The kingdom of God has come near to you." (The seventy are sent out)

32] <u>Luke 17:15</u> "And one of them, when he saw that he was healed, returned, and with a loud voice glorified God,"

33] <u>John 10:10</u> "The thief does not come except to steal, and to kill, and to destroy. I have come that they may have life, and that they may have *it* more abundantly."

34] <u>Acts 4:29-31</u> "Now Lord, look on their threats, and grant to Your servants that with all boldness they may speak Your Word, (30)by stretching out Your hand to heal, and that signs and wonders may be done through the name of Your Holy Servant Jesus." (31)And when they had prayed, the place where they were assembled together was shaken; And they were all filled with the Holy Spirit, and they spoke the Word of God with boldness."

35] <u>Romans8:11</u> " But if the Spirit of Him who raised Jesus from the dead dwells in you, He who raised Christ from the dead will also give life to your mortal bodies through His Spirit who dwells in you."

36] <u>James 5:14-16</u> "Is anyone among you sick? Let him call for the elders of the church, and let them pray over him, anointing him with oil in the name of the Lord. (15)And the prayer of faith will save the sick, and the Lord will raise him up. And if he has committed sins, he will be forgiven. (16) Confess your trespasses to one another, and pray for one another, that you may be healed. The effective, fervent prayer of a righteous man avails much."

37] Revelation 22:2 "In the middle of its street, and on either side of the river, was the tree of life, which bore twelve fruits, each tree yielding its fruit every month. The leaves of the tree were for the healing of the nations."

38] Luke 8:47 "Now when the woman saw that she was not hidden, she came trembling; And falling down before Him, she declared to Him in the presence of the people the reason she had touched Him and how she was healed immediately."

39] Luke 8:48 "And He said to her, 'Daughter, be of good cheer; your faith has made you well. Go in peace.'"

40] Luke 5:17 "Now it happened on a certain day, as He was teaching, that there were Pharisees and teachers of the law sitting by, who had come out of every town of Galilee, Judea, and Jerusalem. And the power of the Lord was present to heal them."

Notes

On this page take the time to examine how you may relate to the chapter you have just read. How will you be able to utilize the points made in this chapter? How will you apply them to your actions and your daily decisions? In healing, it is so important to stop lying to yourself. Be honest, this is between you and God. Remember God loves you, no matter what you believe. If you will be honest with yourself you will be healed by applying these simple but painful truths to your life. Don't give up push through!

_____
_____
_____
_____
_____
_____
_____
_____
_____
_____
_____
_____
_____
_____
_____
_____
_____
_____
_____
_____
_____
_____
_____
_____

Chapter 7

Forgiveness

By Debra Ann Sutterfield

In order to receive salvation we had to be forgiven by Christ. He offers forgiveness freely. The only way to be healed and have victory is by the same token of forgiveness. Your's! Don't quit now. Read on and see how it affected me. Your's is the victory.

The word forgiveness means *freedom, pardon, deliverance, liberty*, and *remission*.

We have talked about "Fake It Til You Make It" and "Before You Can Heal, You Have To Learn To Love Yourself," but the most important thing we will probably discuss is forgiveness. If you truly want happiness, forgiveness is where you have to go.

Coming from a life filled with disappointments, heartbreaks, abuse, neglect and pain, forgiveness is one of the most difficult demands we will make of ourselves. At least, it was for me. In my story, forgiveness was the most difficult thing for me to do in my life. I held grudges, I had true un-forgiveness in my heart. Oh, I called it everything except un-forgiveness. I called it protecting myself so I couldn't be hurt again. I said I didn't hate them, but I did. It didn't matter what I called it. It was un-forgiveness!

John 8:32
Ye shall know the truth and the truth shall make you free.

Until I was honest with myself, I could not learn to forgive. The cold hard fact was that I couldn't forgive those who hurt me. I couldn't forgive myself. How in this world could I believe God would forgive me? I harbored so much animosity in me, so much ill will, so much hate, until I could not have joy in my life. I was sick, physically sick, more often than I was well. I had everything from migraines to depression.

I went to visit a famous iridologist in Kentucky. An iridologist is someone who is trained to look into your eyes and diagnose medical problems. This man is amazing at his job. Usually in about five minutes, he can tell you things that your doctor has to guess at and draw blood for specific tests for until they figure out the problem. On one of my visits, he looked in my eyes and said you have un-forgiveness in your heart. I immediately closed both eyes. I knew he had seen into my soul. I am very blessed that he was a Christian, but I didn't want to hear the truth. He asked, "what, would you do if Jesus didn't forgive you?" I answered, sarcastically (sarcasm was typical in those days), "but Jesus can walk on water and I can't do that either." Pretty much everyone who knew me was aware of my lack of ability to forgive. In my heart, I could kill all affection for that person. I was angry and carried a rage in me that was beyond a description of words.

Un-forgiveness ruled my life. It controlled things I did and events I attended. I just couldn't bring myself to be in the company of some people. I called myself a Christian, but I was full of hatred. Man, it really hurts when you do a reality check on yourself, when you look deep into your own heart, and see the ugliness inside. I had carried that around inside of me for so many years, it was almost like an old friend - a destructive friend, but one I chose to keep.

The word Christian means "like Christ." When Jesus was arrested, Peter cut off the ear of one of the Roman soldiers. Jesus, knowing they were going to crucify him, knowing he could have called a league of angels to save him, he instructed Peter to put away his sword. John 18:10 Forgiveness!

Christ's last words consisted of "Father forgive them." He was tortured and beaten until he was unrecognizable. Yet he was worried about the people being forgiven. He gave his life forgiving me.

Jesus forgives all of the selfish, hateful and uncaring stupid things I do, when I ask for forgiveness. I would always say "well they haven't asked me to forgive them." Jesus forgave his persecutors without them asking, he even said, "for they know not what they do." Maybe, the ones who hurt us don't know they hurt us or don't know how to say I'm sorry, or, maybe, they have as many problems as we do.

Am I so much better than Jesus? Are you? I was putting myself higher than the creator by being the prosecutor, judge and jury. I believed in my heart that, if I forgave someone, it would open me up for more pain. You don't have to associate with them but you do have to forgive them, that is if you want to be healthy and happy and be forgiven by God. Satan wants us to believe the lies and hold onto the grudge that we harbor inside. He wants to remind us how bad that person has been to us and how terribly we were wounded. Satan's greatest goals are to keep us bound in the past and in the un-forgiveness state. He will go so far as to, when we start stepping out on the faith that God has healed us, Satan will start reminding us of our past.

The way Satan continues to keep us in his clutches and in his contract to hell is to keep us in the past. One lie Satan uses on a regular basis is that we ourselves were not forgiven. You see, God does forgive us, but we have to turn away from our sinful actions when we ask for that forgiveness. We have to change our actions. We have to quit believing the lies Satan has been keeping us bound with. If we ever want victory in our life, we have to quit believing Satan! If you want victory, then start living victoriously today!

Daniel 9:9
To the Lord our God belong mercies and forgivenesses, though we have rebelled against him;

God has mercy on us and wants to forgive us, but we have to ask.

Acts 26:18
To open their eyes, and to turn them from darkness to light, and from the power of Satan unto God, that they may receive forgiveness of sins, and inheritance among them which are sanctified by faith that is in me.

If we want to come out of the darkness, depression, illness, and panic, we have to open our eyes and realize first we have to forgive others, and then ask God to forgive us.

Jesus said in Matthew 6:14
For if ye forgive men their trespasses, your heavenly Father will also forgive you.

So we know we have to forgive, but what happens if we forgive and they hurt us again? Well, this is what Jesus said when Peter asked the question.

Matthew 18:21,22
21 Then came Peter to him, and said, Lord, how

oft shall my brother sin against me, and I forgive him? till seven times?
22 Jesus saith unto him, I say not unto thee, Until seven times: but, Until seventy times seven.

Wow, we have to forgive them every time. I said earlier that you do not have to associate with someone who continues to hurt you, but you do have to forgive them. I want to say that if you are in danger of physical harm, get out of that situation. Protect yourself! There are many local agencies that are available both for housing protection and for counseling. If you are involved in an abusive relationship, get help and get out. We have the power to change who we are by refusing to give Satan power over us. Claim victory over your life now! Start today!

The word forgiveness represents freedom. But how do we begin? First, let's **not** look at it as impossible to be forgiven. Don't say, "yes but you don't know what he has done to me", or "let me tell you what she has done." It is not our responsibility to punish. We are expected to forgive. I will say again, because of the importance of it, forgiveness is the beginning of the healing process. Without forgiveness, you will not find joy. When we think of the un-forgiveness we have, we want to justify it. Don't.

There was a popular song a few years ago that went something like this "do it, just do it". Forgive - just do it. Forgiveness is, in essence, the basis of your healing, your happiness, and your freedom.

Make a list of the people you have in your heart that you have un-forgiveness toward. I must warn you that your list is probably longer than you think. Please don't forget to put your name on that list. Now, here is where we put it into action. A friend and mentor to me in Nashville led me through this exercise.

Sitting in Betty's living room, she led me through these words. I had to insert the name into the blank. What happened seemed like it would be an easy task, but it was like tearing down a dam. There were people I did not want to forgive. That sounds silly. I mean, what is the harm in forgiving someone? But, when I said the first name, and then Betty repeated the statement again, as if she knew there was more than one, I stammered, and another name then another. I really don't know how many there were, but there were plenty. It was like water gushing out of that dam. The tears were streaming down my face, and I was sobbing. I had no clue that this was opening the door for victory in my life, but something was happening. All of a sudden I was pouring the statement out on my own with more and more names.

Now, it is time for you to do the same. Trust me, as bad as you don't want to do this, it will change your ability to love yourself and others. Repeat these words and insert the name that comes to your mind. Do it over and over again until you have no one left. If you aren't sure if you feel that way about someone, just throw them in for good measure. It is best to be sure. One more step - say the statement one more time, but this time **insert your name**. Yes, it is important to forgive yourself. Don't feel guilty about whose name you call out. This is between you and God. It may be people you think you shouldn't feel this way about, but it's ok. It is most important to learn to forgive.

Be sure to pray before you begin. Your prayer may begin like this:

Heavenly Father, I love you. Thank you for loving me. Thank you for forgiving me of my sins as I learn to forgive those who have sinned against me. Please cleanse my heart and make me who you designed me to be. Thank you for tearing down the walls of destruction in my life. But most of all God, thank you for loving me so much that you sacrificed your son for my salvation. Help me learn to love like you. Continue to lead me to freedom and joy that I may be able to lead others in the same path to you. Thank you God; Amen

Here is your statement:

I cancel the curse and break the assignment of un-forgiveness against _____ in my life.

Example: I cancel the curse and break the assignment of un-forgiveness against *(insert name of person you are forgiving)* in my life.

Forgiveness Assignment
What Forgiveness Means To You

Colossians 3:13
King James Version (KJV)
13 Forbearing one another, and forgiving one another,
if any man have a quarrel against any: even as Christ
forgave you, so also do ye.

Read the following scriptures and write what they
speak to you.

Mark 11:25-26 Necessity of forgiveness

_____

_____

_____

_____

_____

_____

_____

_____

_____

Matthew 18:21-35 Instructions about forgiveness

_____

_____

_____

_____

_____

_____

_____

_____

Luke 7:40-50 The Parable of the two Debtors

_____

_____

_____

_____

_____

_____

_____

_____

_____

_____

_____

Mark 2:1-12 (Matthew 9:1-8) A paralytic is healed

_____

_____

_____

_____

_____

_____

_____

_____

_____

Matthew 6:9-15 The Lord's Prayer

_____

_____

_____

_____

_____

_____

_____

_____

Tell in your own words how important forgiveness is in your life

_____
_____
_____
_____
_____
_____
_____
_____
_____
_____
_____

Is there room for improvement for forgiving in your life and in what areas would you like to forgive?

_____
_____
_____
_____
_____
_____
_____
_____
_____
_____
_____
_____
_____
_____
_____
_____
_____
_____
_____

<u>Notes</u>

On this page take the time to examine how you may relate to the chapter you have just read. How will you be able to utilize the points made in this chapter? How will you apply them to your actions and your daily decisions? In healing, it is so important to stop lying to yourself. Be honest, this is between you and God. Remember God loves you, no matter what you believe. If you will be honest with yourself you will be healed by applying these simple but painful truths to your life. Don't give up push through!

_____

_____

_____

_____

_____

_____

_____

_____

_____

_____

_____

_____

_____

_____

_____

_____

_____

_____

_____

_____

Chapter 8

Believing in God's Love
Donna's Story

By Donna Story

[16] For God so loved the world, that he gave his only begotten Son, that whosoever believeth in him should not perish, but have everlasting life. **John 3:16** King James Version (KJV)

We live our lives every day, making choices. When we make bad choices, there is a price we have to pay. I thank God every day that I am not defined by the choices I have made. His Word in my life is what defines me. But, we have to agree that we live by those choices we make. This is my testimony of how God has delivered me and brought me through. I thank God for His love that never fails.

I was brought up in a Christian home, saved at the age of 13, but didn't always live my life for Christ. I had two loving parents and 5 sisters. My oldest sister, I hated her, but our house was full of love. We were taught good morals, good work ethic, and how to be kind and compassionate to others.

Hating someone or loving them is a choice we make. Every day that we live, we are making choices. As babies, we choose to learn how to walk. We learn what yes and no means, and we choose how many times we get our hands slapped for reaching for things we shouldn't. As we grow older, we choose to do our homework at school or study for a test. We choose the friends we hang out with. We find that the choices we make influence the rest of our lives. Sometimes our choices are so second nature to us that we find ourselves saying, "what choice did I have?" That's a cop out. We need to look before we leap.

God had to work forgiveness in my life over and over because of the choices I made. Hating my sister, God delivered me when I was in my 30's. God turned my hate to love and gave me a blessing. One of the next major choices I made, right out of high school, was to allow a boy to sweep me off my feet. We had sex outside of marriage. Instead of asking God to help me to repent, I compounded my mistake. I felt so guilty that I thought the only way to fix things so no one would know was to marry the guy when he asked. Oh, what an ugly web we weave when first we set out to deceive. The one I was deceiving was myself and the man I married. Two years later, we had a daughter. She is the most precious gift, next to salvation, that God has blessed me with. I wanted our marriage to work, but neither one of us were happy. He starting getting mad all the time and would slap me, and it went from there into beatings. I thought, there must be something terribly wrong with me for him to act that way. I asked God to help me, but I wasn't serving Him, so why would He want to help. I got myself in the mess so I had to fix it.

We went to church together for a while, but that just seemed to give him fuel to beat me more. One day he almost hit our daughter with a big glass mixing bowl he had thrown at me, and I knew, at that point, it was time to leave. I also found out he was cheating on me. Now I had a biblical reason I could leave on. I didn't learn until our daughter was 21 what an evil monster he was.

A year after divorcing him, I met husband my second husband. We had been together three months when he announced at the supper table that I had to get rid of my daughter. I asked him if he was crazy. He said, "No!" He had a daughter two years older than mine and he wanted me to focus on her. The hurt look on my little girl's face broke my heart. To protect her, I locked us in my bedroom. The next day a judge granted me and annulment right on the spot to protect my daughter.

I don't know why I wanted another man in my life, but I was looking. Before long I met my third husband in a bar. I had asked God why I wasn't able to find a good man, one who loved Him, loved children, and would love me. This is the first time I had included God in a choice of mine. Then as I looked up, the room full of people parted just like the Red Sea and a man at the very end of the room looked up and came my way. He asked me to dance and the rest is history. We lived together for two years. I so thought he was the right man. He loved me, my daughter, and God. We were together for 18 years. At some point, we started going to church. Messenger Chapel was home from the moment I walked in. It was here that I was introduced to the Holy Ghost, and my life was never the same. When we invite the Holy Ghost into our lives, He starts cleaning us up. From this point on, our choices need to be considered because we truly are representing our God.

It was during this time that God told me, if I wanted His forgiveness, I had to forgive. We had some long talks about this. I had gotten real comfortable with the hate and anger in my life. I wasn't sure I wanted to get rid of them. After more talks and reading His Word, I knew He would help me lay these feelings down. I knew, that if I didn't allow Him to do this work in me, I would be miserable. God teaches us what we need to know and helps us make those changes in our lives as we grow closer to Him. So, down the road of forgiveness I went.

My first encounter was with my older sister. We had hated each other for so long, I didn't know how to approach this. God made a way where there seemed to be no way. We were civil to each other around our parents, otherwise we just avoided each other. But, one day my mom called and said this sister had come home for a visit without her family, and she was wishing to save some money and wondered if she could spend the night with us as she passed through. I was shocked, but knew God was opening a door. She came, we talked, we both forgave, and God did a good work. Sometimes forgiveness is not just about forgiving, but about saying we are sorry and asking someone to forgive us for a wrong we did to them.

My next stop was when my parents had refused to sign my papers to join the Peace Corps when I graduated. I was so hurt and angry that I disobeyed them when I married the first time. I had to tell them I was sorry, and I forgave them and asked them to forgive me. They hadn't even realized how much they had hurt me. They said they were sorry I got hurt but not for the decision they had made. Because we talked and forgave, we have a better relationship today.

At this time I had to forgive my first husband for the abuse he put me through. That was a lot harder to do. I knew God would help me through it. I didn't know if I should talk to him, but before I could find him, I received a phone call from his sister-in-law that he had died. I was glad I didn't have to face him because I wasn't sure I could. I told God I forgave him and hoped he had repented so he could make heaven his home. I realized that God had lifted a great burden from me and my daughter when this man had died. The last time we saw him, I told him he wasn't going to disappoint our daughter again by not showing up to get her on his weekends. If he didn't want to be a good dad, my current husband was willing to take over that spot in her life willingly. He said I could do what I wanted, but he knew where we were and I should watch my back.

All those years, we lived in fear, not knowing if he might snatch our daughter or kill one of us. After he died, we had gone shopping in the city. As we walked around in the mall, holding her hand, (what teenager does that, right?) when we looked at each other and realized we didn't have to watch anymore or hold hands. God had freed us from the bondage of fear. A couple of years later my daughter started having seizures. The doctors couldn't find anything wrong and said they were most likely brought on by stress. But, she wouldn't talk to anyone and said she was fine.

One day, while at work, my daughter said she was going to kill herself. The fireman who heard her called the police and they picked her up. Because they knew us, they brought her home and told us she had a choice to be locked up for 48 hours or go to a psychiatric clinic. She made the choice to go to the clinic. I told her, if she didn't talk to the doctors and be honest with them, they wouldn't be able to help her. At the clinic, they told me there would be no contact for 3 days, and then they would call with a progress report and set up visitation times and times if they wanted to include me in any of her sessions. So, I was surprised when the next morning they called and asked if I could come that afternoon and if I could bring my best friend. My friend was also my pastor's wife, so I assumed my daughter might be in need of some spiritual guidance.

How many of you know when God is doing a work in our lives that Satan tries to come in and destroy it? I thought my daughter was finally reaching out in the right direction. She had been brought up in church, and even when I wasn't faithful, she was. But, it seemed like when she realized she didn't need to hold my hand anymore, she let go of God's, too. That afternoon we went to visit, but they asked my friend to stay in the visitors lounge. Nothing could have prepared me for what happened next. The doctor came and got me, took me to a little room with 3 chairs. My daughter came in and sat next to the doctor, and I sat across from them. The doctor told my daughter to share with me what they had talked about after she first got there. She said, "Mom, do you remember when I was about 10 and I would cry because my dad hadn't showed up to get me? Well, I cried because God had spared me another time of having to go with him. Mommy, from the time I was 3 until you told him not to come anymore, he had been molesting me." I couldn't believe what I had just heard. I had lived all her life trying to protect her. What had I done?

I fell out of my chair, covered my head with my arms and screamed and cried, and cried and cried. The doctor finally touched my arm and helped me back into my chair. I couldn't get myself under control, I shook so badly. The doctor said, "so you knew nothing about this?" I looked at my daughter and said, "I didn't. You always knew I would have done anything to protect you. I would have killed him for you!" She told me she couldn't tell me because he had told her, that if she ever told anyone, he would kill me. She had witnessed more of my beatings and what he had done to me than

I knew. So she believed his threats. He had told her, if he had to kill me, no one else loved her and he would be able to do what he wanted to her and no one would care. So, all her life, she was protecting me. What an evil, ugly thing he had done to our daughter. I didn't even have the satisfaction that now that I knew, I couldn't hunt him down, and kill him because he was already dead. I was so angry. He had gotten away with so much and we didn't get to see him punished for any of it. God, how fair was that? I had told myself, and even my daughter, that I could forgive her dad for what he had done to me. But, I couldn't forgive him for what he had done to her. I hurt so much for her, but didn't know how to fix her hurt. She said, if her dad got into heaven, she didn't want to go there. My friend came with me so she could drive me home. She told me to put it in God's hands and let Him comfort us.

My world was crumbling. All the good God had been working in my life was gone. Oh, I still went to church, but I didn't want God working in my life, telling me what I needed to do to draw closer to Him. Over the next few years, my life with my third husband was falling apart. I found out he had been cheating on me. He told me about it and asked me to forgive him. I didn't think I could, and he went back to drinking and drugs. I told him we needed to get some help in order to save our marriage. So we went to my pastor, and the first thing he told him was that everything was my fault because I was having a homosexual relationship with my boss. The pastor asked me if that was true. He and his wife were my friends, how could he ask me that? I was so hurt I left and just gave up. We got a divorce.

I dropped out of church and turned my back on

God. I stopped running with my church family and started running with my friends in the world. I let their lifestyles become mine. I had been trying to get them into church and now nothing was going right. When you run with the world, they will drag you down, but it was my choice. I stopped listening to the voice of God.

I thought I had something to prove, so I became involved with another man. We had been friends for a long time. Our families knew each other. His marriage had fallen apart a year before mine did. We had a few dates, and a year later, we moved in together. We had fun together and enjoyed each other's company. We were friends with fringe benefits. This went on for five years. I was at the point where working hard, playing hard and living in sin was taking its toll on my body. I hurt all the time.

About that time a friend of a friend started working with me. She was a Christian. She watched me every day and saw how I was hurting and told me I wasn't going to change anything until I got my life right with God. She knew the struggles I had gone through with my third husband and was also a friend of my current boyfriend. I loved him, and we were good together. I didn't know how I could get back to God while living in sin. Neither one of us wanted to get married. His only marriage had lasted 37 years, and he had wanted it to be for life. I had three failed marriages and didn't want to add a fourth.

This friend kept asking me to go to church with her. I kept saying, I'd like to, but just wasn't sure. I found myself talking to God once again. He gently led me by telling me the story of the prodigal son and told me, just like him, I could come home. I knew what I had to do. One Wednesday night, I found myself going back to Messenger Chapel. Pastor Jennings was there at that time, and I asked if I could talk to him sometime. He told me right after church that night was fine. I told him everything about quitting church, about my current boyfriend and how I wanted to repent and get my life back on track with God once again. I just wasn't sure what to do. He told me to go home and talk to my boyfriend and be honest with him and let God guide me.

I did as pastor suggested. As I told my boyfriend how I felt a look of relief came on his face that surprised me. I asked him what he thought. I told him we needed to be honest with each other because I wasn't trying to hurt him; I just wanted something better in our lives. He said we had a lot of decisions to make, and we needed to pray about them. He said we already knew we didn't want to get married, and he knew we were living in sin and he felt as guilty about it as I did. He said he would like to have a better relationship with God, too. We talked about moving out, about our finances, and where to go from this point. Our friendship was more important than letting all of this destroy that. Before one of us could find another place to live, his health became bad. I talked to God about what to do, but I did not feel led to leave him to deal with all this on his own. So we stayed together as friends. We were friends sharing an apartment and helping each other, but no more fringe benefits. We let friends and family know what we had decided so there wouldn't be any misunderstandings.

I remember sitting in my chair one night reading my Bible. He was watching TV from his hospital bed. I started laughing. He looked over at me and said, "I didn't know the Bible had anything that funny in it." So I told him how God had been dealing with me and that the scriptures He led me to read were exactly what He had been telling me. He said "sure wish I had that kind of relationship with God." He had been raised Catholic, and it had been all about religion and traditions, but not much about building a personal relationship with Jesus. I told him it was as easy as repenting in his heart for his sins, accepting Jesus as his Savior, and letting God help him change his life. He felt like it was too late for him. I told him, until we take our last breath, we have hope. We turned the television to a church channel, and the preacher was talking about the same thing I had told him. God had been dealing with me, and he used the same scriptures. He was stunned.

A few days later while watching TV, a preacher ended his message by offering to say the sinners prayer with anyone who would like to take Jesus as their Savior. He looked at me and said he was ready. So together, with hands stretched out, we said the sinners' prayer and he received salvation. He was a changed man. He never did make it to church with me. He was afraid his health wouldn't let him sit that long. But, he was sure of his salvation, and we talked about and read the Bible together a lot. God wasn't through with me yet.

God was working something new in me, and I didn't know how much I liked it. He had placed in my heart that I could get married, and it would be a good one because we had Him in our lives. For six years we had shared our lives as just friends, and I didn't know if I wanted to go that direction of committing my life as a wife again. But, I also knew God was working changes in our lives. I told God, that if He was changing my attitude about marriage, He would have to change his, too, because I wasn't going to talk him about it. I asked God what I was supposed to do to further the cause without talking about it. I wanted God's will for me, not my own. God told

That night, as I lay in bed, my question was, where do I go from here, Lord? I knew there was a change to take place, but if marriage wasn't going to happen, what was I to do? I had to trust in God's plan for me and just allow Him to lead me. The very next day he died. Do you know how horrible I felt? It's like I killed him because there was no other direction for us to go. I asked God, why couldn't it have been me. I was ready. He told me he was ready too. I was kind of lost for a couple of weeks, and then I allowed God to comfort me. I still didn't know what to do or where to go. I felt like I was drifting and no help in sight to let me know what direction I needed to go. How was I going to make it on my own? I had a nice long talk with God, and He told me things about us I needed to hear. He told me to return to my first love. I told Him I didn't even know where that person was. God said, "No, not the person you first loved but the One who first loved you." God said, ""I will be your husband, the head of your home, your covering."

I came to a big a-ha moment right then. That's who God had always wanted to be in my life and the relationship He wanted to have with me. So far my relationship with Him had been on my terms. I only went to Him when I couldn't handle things on my own. Otherwise I kept Him in this nice little box. I asked God why my three marriages had failed. He told me it was because I hadn't asked Him if these men were right for me, or I hadn't even asked Him to be the center of those relationships. I said, "what about my third husband?" I had sent up a prayer before I met him. God told me He gave me the best considering where I was. These song words came to mind, looking for love in all the wrong places. I asked God to forgive me for not letting Him be in my choices and for not making Him the center of my life. We talked about our relationship and where I wanted it to go from this point. It was like He was asking me to marry Him and to be His only. I had to make the choice to say yes or no. I read the Bible because I just couldn't wrap my brain around being married to God and Him being my husband. The scriptures He led me to read were His love story to me. At last, I had found my one true love. He spoke of all He would do for me. He said He had already given His life for me. He told me all the wonderful things a woman wants to hear from the person who professes his love to the one he wants to spend all his life with.

He has given us His Word and has written it down so everyone can see the promises He made to us. He sealed those words with the precious blood of Jesus just to let us know how serious He is about the relationship we can have together. He wants to be everything to us. He wants to be in every aspect of our lives. There is nothing too small or too big that He can't handle. Over the last three years I have been having so much fun learning about God's love for me.

He is with me no matter what I am doing or where I go. He helps me with my finances; He goes shopping with me. He goes to work with me. He never fails me or leaves me. He doesn't get mad at me if I forget to include Him, but gently reminds me to never shut Him out because, after all, He only wants good for me. How awesome is my God? As I learn more about God's love for me, the more I want others to know about Him. I want to share His love with others as He shares with me. I want so much for my daughter to know this special love God has for each of us, His creation.

I still haven't worked through all the forgiveness God wants me to give to those who have hurt me. God helped me to see how my pastor had done what he had to do to show my third husband, that just because he was my friend, he would be impartial in counseling us. I knew I had to talk to him and tell him I was sorry for how I had handled things and ask his forgiveness. That went well.

Then God told me I had to forgive my first husband for what he had done to me and my daughter. I still knew I could forgive him for myself, but for what he had done to our daughter, I just wasn't so sure about. I wanted to, and God knew it my heart. He gave me some words to share with my daughter. I asked her, "You know God loves us all, because He created us? I know you said you don't want to go to heaven if God forgave your dad, and he is now in heaven. God said to ask you if you could remember just one good thing about your dad?" She said, "well, I remember how we tried to surprise you one time and made some cookies together." Is there anything else you can remember? "What about the time you wanted to make him dinner and you put a clump of peanut butter on a piece of bread and a clump of mayo on another piece of bread and smashed them together and he ate every bite and told you how good it was?" She got just a hint of a smile. "Who taught you to ride a horse?" By the time we got through remembering good times, we were laughing. Now she had a smile on her face.

I said, "When someone repents of their sins, they are forgiven. It doesn't mean we forget what they have done. God say's, that if your dad made it into heaven and you choose to go there, that when you see him you won't know him by the bad he did, because those things don't go to heaven. You'll know him by the goodness that was in him. In heaven you won't hurt, you won't cry there, there will only be joy and happiness. Isn't that what God tells us in His Word?"

I was trying to convince her to forgive, but I still was trying to deal with the wanting to kill him thing myself. I wanted to be able to totally forgive him myself. I told God how I felt and how I needed His help, (we shouldn't want to do anything without His help). God gave me a dream. The dream let me see how our lives would have turned out if she had told me what her dad was doing and that our story would have been more horrible than either of us could have imagined at the time. God eventually allowed me to share this dream with my daughter. It's all in God's timing to do a work and not in our own. This is what I shared:

You know that every day we make choices? Some choices are good, and some are bad. But we have to live with those choices. Your dad made a lot of bad choices. God couldn't stop him because God gave us free will. God hopes we will make choices that are good, but when we don't, they don't just affect our lives, but so many others that we don't even consider when we do make a choice. Do you always make good choices? I know you don't because of how I see you live your life and how your choices affect your daughter. But that doesn't stop God from loving you. He wants only good for His children and hopes we will turn to Him when we have a decision to make. You had to make choices at age three that you shouldn't have had to make. When you chose to not tell me what your dad was doing, God worked in that choice and protected you from far worse. I told her about my dream and how God had worked in me to forgive her dad. Please forgive God, and let Him work forgiveness in you towards your dad too. I had to trust God's words would get through to her. She told me she would have to think about it.

When we started this group, "Jewels in the Sand," I came to realize I had not forgiven myself for the part I had played in this situation between my daughter and her dad. I hadn't told her I was sorry or asked her to forgive me. I blamed myself for not seeing what had been going on and for not protecting her from such evil. I thank God He always makes a way for us to do the things He wants us to accomplish when we aren't sure when or how to do them. A couple of weeks ago I went to spend some time with my daughter. When I got there she said she needed to pick her daughter up from her dad's and wanted to know if I wanted to ride along. We had four hours before we got back to her home to talk. I told her, that in everything that had happened to her in the past, I had forgotten to tell her how sorry I was for not being able to protect her and asked if she could forgive me, too. She said, "Mom, you were as much a victim as I was, and we both did what we needed to do to protect each other, not knowing everything. I love you and don't blame you for any part of that bad past. After you told me the dream God gave you, I'm glad I made the choice I did to not tell you." She said she was glad I had explained about heaven and how she would see her dad for only the good, but she still wasn't sure about forgiving him, she was working on it. She was glad that we hadn't had to live through worse and that neither one of us had to kill him. She thought maybe dying as he did was us seeing his punishment. She still is not sure about everything she felt, but I know with God's love and help they will work it out.

I know now I can truly put this in my past. I don't have those feelings of wanting to kill him anymore. I'm glad God took care of all that for me. When I have to tell my story now, and the more I tell it, the less pain I will feel from the remembering. In ministering God's words to my daughter, He also ministered to me. There is now a new look in my daughters eyes that I hadn't seen for over 30 years. I'm expecting great things in her life as she allows God to be a part of it.

In the beginning, God created the heaven and the earth. And the earth was without form, and void and darkness was on the face of the deep. And the Spirit of God moved upon the face of the waters. And God said, "Let there be light."

Will you allow God's light to shine in your life? Will you allow Him to become your husband? I have learned, that my God is all about relationships, mainly, ours with Him. He knows what we need, and He wants only good for us. We'll always be going through good times and bad, but whatever it is, He will be there for us. His Word says He will never leave us nor forsake us. We are to be thankful in all things. Give your choices over to Him and He will help us through anything we face. Without Him, it is a lonely road that only leads us to destruction. God never stops loving us, but He wants us to look before we leap. Think what each choice will bring you. Let God's Spirit guide you in that choice.

Your homework for this week: here is a list of scriptures to read. See how they speak to you of God's love: Psalm 139, Isaiah 54:5--all of the 'Song of Solomon', all of the book of 'James', John 3:14-21, I Corinthians 13:1-13, and Matthew 22:36-40.

Write down things you want to remember and reflect on them over time. God bless you!

KNOWING WHO GOD IS

These are the different names for God that are found in the Bible and there meanings and the scriptures where they are found:

1] ELOHIM - Genesis 1:1
In the beginning God created the heavens and the earth.

2] EL ELYON - Genesis 14:18-20
Then Melchizedek king of Salem brought out bread and wine; he was the priest of God Most High. And he blessed him and said: "Blessed be Abram of God Most High, Possessor of heaven and earth; And blessed be God Most High, Who has delivered your enemies into your hand." And he gave him a tithe of all.

Psalm 57:2
I will cry out to God Most High, to God who performs all things for me.

3] EL ROI - Genesis 16:13
Then she called the name of the Lord who spoke to her, YOU-ARE-the-GOD-WHO-SEES; for she said, "Have I also here seen Him who sees me?"

4] EL OLAM - Genesis 21:33
Then Abraham planted a tamarisk tree in Beersheba, and there called on the name of the Lord, the Everlasting God.

5] JEHOVAH JIRAH - Genesis 22:14

And Abraham called the name of the place, THE-LORD-WILL-PROVIDE; as it is said to this day, "In the Mount of the Lord it shall be provided."

6] JEHOVAH - Exodus 3: "I AM has sent me to you.'"

7] JEHOVAH RAPHA - Exodus 15:26

And said, "If you diligently heed the voice of the Lord your God and do what is right in His sight, give ear to His commandments and keep all His statutes, I will put none of the diseases on you which I have brought on the Egyptians. For I am the Lord who heals you."

8] JEHOVAH NISSI - Exodus 17:15

And Moses built an altar and called its name, THE-LORD-is-MY-BANNER;

9] JEHOVAH SHALOM - Judges 6:24

So Gideon built an altar there to the Lord, and called it THE-LORD-SHALOM. To this day it is still in Ophrah of the Abiezrites.

I Corinthians 14:33
For God is not the author of confusion but of peace, as in all the churches of the saints.

10] JEHOVAH SHAMMAH - Psalm 46:1

God is our refuge and strength, Avery present help in trouble.

Ezekiel 48:35

"All the way around shall be eighteen thousand cubits; and the name of the city from that day shall be: THE LORD is THERE."

11] EL SHADDAI - Psalm 91:1

He who dwells in the secret place of the Most High shall abide under the shadow of the Almighty.

Matthew 6:25-26

Therefore I say to you, do not worry about your life, what you will eat or what you will drink; nor about your body, what you will put on. Is not life more than food and the body more than clothing? Look at the birds of the air, for they neither sow nor reap nor gather into barns; yet you, heavenly Father, feeds them. Are you not of more value than they?

12] JEHOVAH-TSIDKENU - Jeremiah 23:6

In His days Judah will be saved, and Israel will dwell safely; Now this is His name by which He will be called; THE LORD OUR RIGHTEOUSNESS.

Notes

On this page take the time to examine how you may relate to the chapter you have just read. How will you be able to utilize the points made in this chapter? How will you apply them to your actions and your daily decisions? In healing, it is so important to stop lying to yourself. Be honest, this is between you and God. Remember God loves you, no matter what you believe. If you will be honest with yourself you will be healed by applying these simple but painful truths to your life. Don't give up push through!

_____

_____

_____

_____

_____

_____

_____

_____

_____

_____

_____

_____

_____

_____

_____

_____

_____

_____

_____

_____

_____

Chapter 9

How Does Your Garden Grow

By Cecilia Smith

[20] "Go, stand in the temple courts," he said, "and tell the people all about this new life." **Acts 5:20**

New International Version (NIV)

Jesus forgives us of our sins - but, do we? Old Man. New Man.

What's in Your Garden?

Romans 12:2
Do not be conformed to the pattern of this world, but be transformed by the renewing of your mind.

Eph 5:20   1 Thes 5:18
Through our struggles and trials we are strengthened therefore...   give thanks for and in all things

Rev 12:11
"And they overcame him because of the blood of the Lamb and because of the word of their testimony, and they did not love their life even when faced with death."

Have you ever been sick and tired of being sick and tired? Well, from one who came from dire straits of that definition, I dare you to take a change challenge.

You have already taken huge steps - believing who you are in Christ, looking at a real truth of identity as God created you, and remember, God CANNOT lie! You have stepped into the process of forgiveness of self and others which is life-long. With that, and following along with that of "putting on the new man" (or women, in this case) is taking off the old. There is a time and a place, and, yes, even a use for the old. But, let us remember the example of the wine skin, we cannot put new wine into an old wineskin. So, let us learn how to allow the Holy Spirit to be our guide in directing us toward using our past from our "mess" into our "message."

Revelations 12:11 tells us, by the blood of the Lamb and the word of our testimonies, yes, the Word of God, but, it is also our own testimony. Our story is the only one we have to tell, so let us use what the enemy sought as our destruction as his own defeat!

Turn it right back around on him ladies and TAKE BACK YOUR TERRITORY! WAGE WAR! For the battle is not against flesh, but rather against powers and principalities (Ephesians 6:12). The battle is in our minds! It is a known fact agreed upon by the world, science, and Christianity that the battle is fought not on the ground, but in our minds! It is all controlled in our thought process. Just think upon that for more than a moment, if we are what we think, and we can do what we think (WHAT SCRIPTURE TELLS US, THE TRUTH) then, what mighty warriors we are and how much time and effort we waste on being defeated with worry, sickness, hurt and pain if God is for us then WHO can stand against us? With all that being said, who do we fear, God or man? Are we more worried about what sister Sara said about us, or what God says about us? Are we stuck in what happened to us yesterday, or what Robert did to us last year rather than what wonderful things God has for us today?

I will remember if I change my actions my thoughts will follow. Let us be transformed by the renewing of our minds.

After my mother died, there was an unsettling deep inside me. I had lost my younger brother, then my father, who was my best friend, and then my mom. I was the last of my immediate family, and even though I was married, had children, grandchildren, and many friends, I felt alone. I felt cheated. Lord, why were You allowing all this? All of these families, some very close to me, right in front of me, even children older than me, much older than me, and still had all their parents and even, much less siblings. They didn't even speak, or at most didn't like each other, or acted like it was a chore to talk to one another. Our family loved and enjoyed one another, and we were separated!!!!! I was playing the victim role, wallowing in self-pity, loathing in addictions of all sorts, and looking for answers for self and flesh and justice. Life went on as it does, and so I found myself moving with it. Before long, it was Spring again, and I decided to put in a small garden of flowers and some vegetables and herbs. It wasn't any big garden, nothing special, but something was better than nothing which is what I felt like. It was the beginning of a life lesson for me.

In July, the opportunity to move came out of nowhere and by the end of the month, we were moving. My flowers were an issue. Some people told me that trying to transplant them at this time of year would be a waste of time and they would not survive. Despite all the comments, I was determined to have the garden, especially when I thought of all the coaxing it took to convince my husband to invest his time, sweat, and finances for my enjoyment, and then do it all over again in a month or so later! Still another month later – after a lot, and I mean a LOT of sweat – all but one plant made it and my garden was so much better for all the effort.

I was sitting out on the patio a couple of weeks

later with coffee and Bible, the sunrise was splendid, the fountain was running, the flowers were blooming and God was shining all around me! How awesome is HE! My flower garden - nursing and babying them back after moving them from ground to new ground – higher ground. Fertilizing, watering, all the extra care and attention I had given them trying to coax them back to flourishing health and beauty, the magnificent color, the strength of their stalks and stems, allowed them to produce what God made them to be. How much so God works with us, when He moves us to new ground, to higher ground, when we place our hope and faith in Him, when we trust Him to transplant us (regardless of what circumstances or others say), His outreaching arms, the gentle care of His hands, forming, nurturing, fertilizing coaxing us to grow, to bloom, to produce fruit and blossom. How magnificent His grace, how wonderful His loving care!

Years later, I look back and I see a small part of the picture of that small garden. From that small garden, as I put up salsa and sauce from the tomatoes, and peppers and canned them, giving them to friends and family, selling them at functions, and met some great people and other organizations. As I sit this morning with another great sunrise, another great cup of coffee, that same amazing Bible, and that same AMAZING GOD, I stand in Awe with tears in my eyes in how far God has brought me and my little garden. I can't wait to see what is next and just what He has planted, waiting for me, to harvest inside.
What's in your garden?
How have you helped or hindered your garden to be

planted?
Transplanted?
Harvested?
Used as service?
Shared the harvest?
Shared your testimony?

Thank you, Father, for always being there even when we face new ground. You are there, turning the soil, seeing the new growth, even when we don't. Help us to be thankful as you adjust our roots. Thank you for quenching a thirst that I pray grows and continues in desire for You always. Our hope is in you – our fertilizer. Your finger to direct us toward Your light and path, that we may produce through You and for You, the beautiful blooms and fruit we were made for. Made perfect in You, for You, by You. Thank you Father for a grateful heart. God I thank you for your voice and your promise.

God loves us right where we are and he will lead us to higher ground if we choose to be transplanted. Be renewed and transformed by the renewing of our minds. He will use our past to bring others into the harvest and multiply our garden and to share in our harvest. He will give us multiple blessings by sharing our testimonies and giving him the glory, but he will only do this if we allow him to, not only transplant and grow us, but to use us and share us.

So again how does your garden grow?

Notes

On this page take the time to examine how you may relate to the chapter you have just read. How will you be able to utilize the points made in this chapter? How will you apply them to your actions and your daily decisions? In healing, it is so important to stop lying to yourself. Be honest, this is between you and God. Remember God loves you, no matter what you believe. If you will be honest with yourself you will be healed by applying these simple but painful truths to your life. Don't give up push through!

_____

_____

_____

_____

_____

_____

_____

_____

_____

_____

_____

_____

_____

_____

_____

_____

_____

_____

_____

_____

Chapter 10

Broken to Beauty

By Cecilia Smith

[11] Let the king be enthralled by your beauty;
honor him, for he is your lord God's Promise: **Psalm 45:11**
New International Version (NIV)

Isaiah 61

> The Spirit of the Sovereign Lord is on me,
>   because the Lord has anointed me
>   to proclaim good news to the poor.
> He has sent me to bind up the brokenhearted,
>   to proclaim freedom for the captives
> and release from darkness for the prisoners,[a]
> ² to proclaim the year of the Lord's favor
>   and the day of vengeance of our God,
>   to comfort all who mourn,
> ³and provide for those who grieve in Zion—
>   to bestow on them a crown of beauty
>   instead of ashes,
>   the oil of joy
>   instead of mourning,
>   and a garment of praise
>   instead of a spirit of despair.
> They will be called oaks of righteousness,
>   a planting of the Lord
> for the display of his splendor.   (NIV)

Looking back, some of my darkest places in my life, the most broken depths of me have turned out to be the greatest places of growth and proven God's grace and love as His Glory reigned over me.
My brokenness is raised by Him to beauty, my mess has become a message, testimony, purpose and proof that He exists. My faults and failures maintain

humility. That hole that only He can fill becomes my reminder of life through and with Him. Just like the examples he left through His Word of the adulterers, murderers, liars and thieves. He uses the broken in great and mighty ways – we all are special! Great news! There are no spectators in God's kingdom – without everybody- there is "no body."

Every choice you make brings consequences, either good or bad. When I continued to make bad choices to the point where I dug a huge hole for myself that no one (even if they still chose to be around) could help me. Those proved to be some of my most vital opportunities for growth in Him and in every aspect of my life. These are now the successes I can look back on and the very ones that grow my faith.

It grows my faith by gaining hands on experience with Him. Not only His word tells me, but He is so gracious as to let me experience that trust, time after time. Then time after time, as He proves, I gain trust in Him. So, it makes sense that the times when only God could save me, is by His message found in my mess.

There are a lot of "but GOD" journeys and experiences in my life and I know if you only allow Him to guide and direct you, if you will trust Him, you too will have your own ledger of testimonies of "but GOD".

Start from broken to beauty by receiving where

131

God places you. When you are willing and trust Him enough to walk through the doors of those opportunities. Not one opportunity goes without the substance to make a difference, so, choose to walk through each day in faith and trust as an opportunity to serve Him and be used by Him in great and mighty ways. Trust that you will be led by the Spirit in the right places in the right time, even when, and especially when, they don't make since by your senses (see, touch, taste and feel) or by your natural worldly experience.

To walk through the valleys and the darkness shows us the Truth of light!! You see, it is not about the circumstance, or the falls, no one has walked the earth without trials and troubles. In fact, scripture clearly tells us we <u>will</u> have them.
It is about what you do with and how you respond to the trials, troubles, the darkness and the mistakes that matters.

When I went to jail and then prison, I had a choice on what and who to be right then. That choice didn't have anything to do with my sentence, or what others thought of me. It did have to do with; I was going to do that time one way or the other. I was angry and I had a good old fashioned pit party for myself. The problem was though everyone else was invited, no one came!

So even though I initially made the choice out of anger, I still made a choice that I was going to hold my head up high, do that time to the best of my ability, and to learn and grow from it. That I was going to gain from the experience as dark as it seemed at that moment and use it as an opportunity to spend some time on myself and getting to really know God.

It goes way past religion that is man made to a relationship. To not just know about Him but really know Him like I would any other friend or family member I valued. And so I did. What a wonderful day! It lead to a wonderful one true LIVING GOD, a Savior, helper, confidant, healer, guider, provider, and the great "I AM." I could go on and on but hopefully you get the picture.

I chose to use the experience instead of allowing it to use me. Even if I didn't understand it at the time! It's not all about understanding the situation but it is about trusting Him in all things, which ultimately leads to thanking Him in and for all things. Our Father is the 'Great I AM' who can and will work for you, in you, through you and around you!

Peace in the midst of the storm only comes with practice and experience. It teaches the abundance in true joy and it builds faith in the one who will never leave you or let you down. Grace is given, trust is earned. And the Lord loves me enough, you enough even to the point of allowing us to love in a depth beyond our understanding and test His ways and see He is worthy.

Through our faith, <u>the blood</u> of Jesus Christ IS OUR RIGHTEOUSNESS

Do not put your identity in who you are with your past! In the world, my identity says I am an offender, a drug addict, a felon. I was convicted and sentenced. Regardless of how long ago that was, or if I have served and completed the sentence I was given, I am still identified with those titles.

The Word (my mirror), His truth, who My Father says I am, is a new creation. Sealed in Him through the blood of Jesus Christ, I'm redeemed from that conviction, a child of God, the One True King, and the one true judge.

I am anointed and appointed through that blood and the Word sanctified and sealed. I have a message and a purpose and I will not fail with Him. Through Him I can do all things and have the same power (my born again Spirit) made perfect in Christ who lives in me) that Jesus had and has when He raised the dead! Think about that my beloved! We all have that!

Don't let Satan and his posse, the world, or even those with good intentions, to place your thoughts on anything but the truth.

Proverbs 23:7
... for as a man (woman) thinketh in his heart, so he is.

So again, the price has been paid for your freedom and the deposit has been made in your account for everything you will ever need. Each and every one of us has been given the choice.

What do you choose - Broken or Beauty?

John 8:36
For if the Son sets you free, you will be free indeed! (NIV)

Notes

On this page take the time to examine how you may relate to the chapter you have just read. How will you be able to utilize the points made in this chapter? How will you apply them to your actions and your daily decisions? In healing, it is so important to stop lying to yourself. Be honest, this is between you and God. Remember God loves you, no matter what you believe. If you will be honest with yourself you will be healed by applying these simple but painful truths to your life. Don't give up push through!

_____

_____

_____

_____

_____

_____

_____

_____

_____

_____

_____

_____

_____

_____

_____

_____

_____

_____

_____

_____

_____

Chapter 11

Know What You Know

By Debra Ann Sutterfield

[19] We know that we are children of God, and that the whole world is under the control of the evil one. [20] We know also that the Son of God has come and has given us understanding, so that we may know him who is true. And we are in him who is true by being in his Son Jesus Christ. He is the true God and eternal life. **1John 5:19-20** New International Version (NIV)

We have talked about how the words we use have an impact on how we feel about ourselves. We talked about how important forgiveness is of others and of ourselves. We discussed how we need to love ourselves in order to be able to love others. As we continue our journey of healing, we find it is important to stand on our faith and **know** for sure that what we **know** is true. To do this, we look inside ourselves and inside the word of God and **know** that we can depend on his word to always be honest and true. We need to **know** that his interest in us is more important to us than our own interest in ourselves.

God's interest in us is to prosper us and to have good plans for us. Maybe you are like I was. I thought God did not find favor in me. This thought caused me to struggle, pray, and beg. I had it in my mind that if I could work hard enough to prove myself worthy, God would hear me and answer my prayers. The more I struggled and prayed, the more I realized this didn't work either. You see, God doesn't work like that. I have been using this technique for years trying to find favor from people around me. This technique never worked for me on people, but I was determined to make it work, so I kept trying. I was such a victim, I was hurt, wounded, and depressed. They say, insanity is doing the same thing over and over again expecting different results. If you looked at what I was doing, you would have had to put me in the insane category.

Thank God, one day I made a decision to make a change in me. I decided to work on me. I mean, after all, I couldn't get my husband to love and respect me, and God didn't seem to care, it looked like I was on my own.

Looking back on my twenty one year marriage, I now realize, how could I, expect respect, after all, I had no respect for me. How could I expect God to hear my prayers and answer them when I was so defeated? I _knew_ he wouldn't. All of this being said, back in those days which I refer to as "in my last life," the "**know what I know,**" was all victim mentality. I got exactly what I expected, not what I wanted, but what I expected. Maybe, if I had stopped and taken the time to study the word of God with a different frame of mind, looking for **know**ledge looking to **know**, I might have paid a little attention to "Proverbs 20:15 *There is gold, and a multitude of rubies: but the lips of **know**ledge are a precious jewel.*" I was so hard headed, looking for **know**ledge never entered my mind until God opened a window and flooded my soul with a desire to change.

So, how did I make the change? What did I do to receive God's blessings, to go from victim to victorious? Is it possible that you can change and leave your negativity and pain behind? All of the practices that we have been doing up to this point has seemed like small little steps, but here is where it becomes meaningful. We have to understand that we *know what we know* in full faith and expectation. We must come to the place that we believe the new words we have created about us. We must come to understand that God answers our prayers, when we understand his ways and expectations of us.

Know #1

All things have order, for every action there is a reaction. It doesn't matter if the action is positive or negative, there will be a matching reaction positive or negative. **Know**ing this makes it ever so important to **know** the correct way to pray, to respond to others, and to yourself.

Romans 12:2
And be not conformed to this world: <u>but be ye transformed by the renewing of your mind,</u> that ye may prove what is that good, and acceptable, and perfect, will of God.

Know #2
The depth of your joy will be determined by the depth of your forgiveness. The total amount of joy you have will be controlled by your total amount of forgiveness of others and self. It is extremely important to forgive without punishing.

Matthew 6:14
For if ye forgive men their trespasses, <u>your heavenly Father will also forgive you.</u>

Know #3
What you **know** and believe is what you shall become. If you want to be victorious over your pain, **you must believe** in your heart. It makes no difference what you have been told in the past to tear you down or what has been done to you. **Know** that you can change that belief, into an overcoming child of God belief. If you want a new life, you can have it. No, it is not easy to reprogram who we are into who we want to be, but it can be done if you follow the rules of victory.

Proverbs 23:7
For as he <u>thinketh</u> in his heart, so is he.

Know #4

The enemy comes against us in many ways. He comes as he plants a small doubt in our head, such as "you **know** you aren't really forgiven (worthy, drug free, free of alcoholism, etc.). You may hear that little voice say, "you **know** one little drink won't hurt you" or "one little pill will just take the edge off," or "what harm will one little _____do?"

    Satan also uses people we love to help us believe the lies he wants us to believe about ourselves. These are only a few of the ways Satan, along with his battery of demons, uses to attack us, in an attempt to keep us from victory. If he can attack us in the battlefield of our mind, he **know**s he has a great chance of winning. But, we serve the King of Kings and greater is he than the adversary. Greater is He that lives in me, than he that lives in this world. We must **know** in our heart and mind that, if God says we are worthy, if God says we are free, if God says we are forgiven, then **no one,** not Satan or anyone acting as his advocate, can change that! **God cannot lie!**

2nd Corinthians 10:4-5
[4] (For the weapons of our warfare are not carnal, but mighty through God to the pulling down of strong holds;) [5] Casting down imaginations, and every high thing that exalteth itself against the knowledge of God, and bringing into captivity every thought to the obedience of Christ;

141

Know #5
Romans 12:3
For I say, through the grace given unto me, to every man that is among you, not to think of himself more highly than he ought to think; but to <u>think</u> *soberly, according as God hath dealt to every man the measure of faith.*

Romans 12:3, is scripture that keeps us in line to not place ourselves above others, but to think soundly in faith as to who we are in God. That being said, we must **know** that God made us in his image, he did not make us as junk. You are worthy to receive his blessings if you follow his path he has laid out for you. God has laid this ministry on my heart to help you find his path of righteousness, to help you find victory, to help you rise to leadership to assist other women to overcome their prison. **Know** that God has a plan for you!

Jeremiah 29:11
For I <u>know</u> *the plans I have for you" declares The Lord, "plans to prosper you and not to harm you, plans to give you hope and a future. (NIV)*

Know #6
God has chosen you! He called you to do this workbook. He called you to grow. He called you to be healed. You have not accidentally fallen into this study. You were chosen! Right now, you just want to work on making you ok. But as you grow, you are going to come upon someone who has walked in your path. At that time, you will **know** what to say to encourage them.

God will give you a peace to be able to speak, and you will **know** you have been called.

Jeremiah 29:11
For I know the plans I have for you" declares The Lord, "plans to prosper you and not to harm you, plans to give you hope and a future". (NIV: I love this scripture)

Know #7
Know that God is God! You cannot forget your past, but you can grow strong from it. God will make you like a mighty oak. The oak begins from a tiny acorn, but amazing things happen as it takes roots and begins to grow. The roots grow deep, the tree grows strong, it becomes a mighty oak. It will bend and bow in the wind, but will not break; it will provide shade and comfort to the weary. God will make you like the mighty oak, comforting others and withstanding the storms of life Satan throws at us in an attempt to destroy us. *(1 Peter 5:8 Be sober, be vigilant; because your adversary the devil, as a roaring lion, walketh about, seeking whom he may devour:)* **Know** your strength comes from God and study his word so you may grow.

Proverbs 4:20-22
My son, attend to my words; incline thine ear unto my sayings.
[21] Let them not depart from thine eyes; keep them in the midst of thine heart. [22] For they are life unto those that find them, and health to all their flesh,

To grow and heal to find peace and joy, you must stop **know**ing the lies to be truth. You have to learn what is real. Reprogram yourself to **know what you know!** The truth is **you are** worthy, **you are** a precious jewel, **you are** beautiful, **you are** powerful, **you are** victorious! After all, if you were created in God's image, how could you be anything but worthy, precious, beautiful, powerful and victorious?

Genesis 1:27
So God created man in his own image, in the image of God created he him; male and female created he them.
And verse 28 says *"and God blessed them".*

If you **know what you know,** then **know** the word of God and **know** you are blessed! Isn't it time we start claiming those blessings? It is time to start speaking blessings over ourselves, our children, our homes, our health and our finances. And, if you **know what you know,** then stand in expectations of miracles!

Each day this week write down the truth that you **know that you know** in your life and be amazed at your blessings.

_____

_____
_____
_____
_____
_____
_____
_____
_____
_____
_____
_____
_____
_____
_____
_____
_____
_____
_____
_____
_____
_____
_____
_____
_____
_____
_____
_____
_____
_____
_____
_____
_____
_____

HOW SATAN HOLDS US IN BONDAGE

The words listed below are the things Satan uses to hold us in bondage:

ADDICTIONS	FEAR
STRESS	ANXIETY
INSECURITY	DEPRESSION
UNFORGIVENESS	GUILT
LACK OF IDENTITY	BITTERNESS
HOPE DEFERRED	ANGER
SELF REJECTION	SELF HATRED
BROKEN HEARTED	SHAME

A STRONG NEED TO BE LOVED AND NURTURED

FEAR OF RESPONSIBILITY

ABANDONMENT BY FATHER

OCCULT IN PAST GENERATIONS

The strategy of Satan hasn't changed it is to get you to believe in the lies that you are insecure and inferior, and to get you to walk in rebellion and rejection.

LUKE 2:40

And the child grew, and waxed strong in spirit, filled with wisdom: and the grace of God was upon Him.

Now put your name in place of 'the child' in that verse. Now we should confess the favor of God over our life at all times.

Look up Philippians 3:13-14 (forgetting our past) – Write down how these scriptures speak to you.

_____

_____

_____

_____

_____

_____

_____

_____

_____

_____

_____

_____

_____

_____

_____

_____

_____

_____

_____

Notes

On this page take the time to examine how you may relate to the chapter you have just read. How will you be able to utilize the points made in this chapter? How will you apply them to your actions and your daily decisions? In healing, it is so important to stop lying to yourself. Be honest, this is between you and God. Remember God loves you, no matter what you believe. If you will be honest with yourself you will be healed by applying these simple but painful truths to your life. Don't give up push through!

_____
_____
_____
_____
_____
_____
_____
_____
_____
_____
_____
_____
_____
_____
_____
_____
_____
_____
_____
_____
_____
_____
_____
_____

Chapter 12

Yes, I Am A Princess!

By Amber McKenzie Smith

[8] Henceforth there is laid up for me a crown of righteousness, which the Lord, the righteous judge, shall give me at that day: and not to me only, but unto all them also that love his appearing. **2 Timothy 4:8** King James Version (KJV)

"So, in Christ Jesus, you are all children of God through faith," (Galatians 3:26). If the Lord, our God, is the King of Kings, how then is it possible that we are not all royalty? Are we not all daughters of The Most High God? In fact, we are all his daughters. We are all Princesses and Heiresses to his mighty throne! "If you belong to Christ, then you are Abraham's seed, and heirs according to the promise." (Galatians 3:26). God has blessed each of us just as he has created us. Like any gift in life, you must appreciate and utilize what is given to you to reap its benefits. We must each pick up the crown that our Father has given us and claim our position as Princesses to the King of Kings! With his love, we can conquer anything.

This hypothetical crown, to me, represents every woman's self-worth. We all struggle to see the good-deserving Princesses inside ourselves. It is so easy to self-criticize and critique. As women, we can look in the mirror and find a new problem every day. We obsess with being perfect so often that we are unable to see just how great we are. None of us are more deserving than the next. So why are we so concerned with our own self-image? Why don't we think we are good enough? Why are we such harsh critics? Society and media portray what "good" is supposed to look like. Well ladies, the media is wrong! My God says that a virtuous woman is more precious than rubies and gold. My Bible never mentions a woman's wardrobe, hair, or lack of cellulite as a measure of worth! And, the last time I checked, I was unable to find an expiration date anywhere in my Bible. Our crown, our self-worth, is an entitlement from our God and does not need approval from Joan Rivers or any red carpet mogul.

Personally, I am a great example of a girl who has needed countless reminders that I needed to "get it together" and put on my crown. There have been times where I've needed a swift kick to the seat and someone to mentally shake some sense into my stubborn self. But, for a hard headed mule, as myself, there's never an ample supply of people around whose words and advice give us that swift kick and shake we need. And, if the great advice has been there, chances are it took me years for the words to sink in. More often than not, I've been able to give others great pep talks while ignoring the fact that I should be listening to my own words. In my own personal struggles to wear my Father's crown, I have spent a lot of time with it both covered in mud and choking me.

My mother's unfortunate childhood and battered spirit had a great effect on my childhood. Mom was so damaged by the hands of her father, the words of my father, and the subsequent emotional abandonment that she felt from the world. It was clear that she was determined to compensate every aspect of my life to make up for her own. We all know that "fixing" someone else doesn't "fix" you, but she was determined to try. I was greatly blessed by her efforts to. Every day of my life, I was told how beautiful I was. Subsequently I was a ham and loved the attention.

Telling me I was beautiful wasn't good enough for mom. She put me in every beauty pageant around because, unlike her, I was going to be convinced I was beautiful. I had an entire room full of trophies and crowns and titles as high as "Little Miss Georgia." I wanted to dance as a child so, I didn't just dance I danced tap, jazz, and ballet. Somehow in this busy schedule, I still got to go to gymnastics, because in her heart, I deserved the best. I wanted to learn music, so she bought me a piano an abundance of lessons. I could read and write at three-years-old because she spent every waking hour ensuring that I was the best. And being the daughter of the Sunday School director, she also blessed me with a strong Christian foundation. I'm certain my mother deserved some sort of award for her valiant efforts.

When I was in second grade, I began to become aware of my parents' fighting. I would sit with my ear to my bedroom door to hear every word. They said such mean things to each other. As an adult, I know that they weren't mean people, but people who were raised to communicate with anger and defensiveness. As a child I wasn't so wise. All I did is listen to the words and take them to heart. I remember sitting on my bed wearing my pageant crowns. I would stare in the mirror and imagine I was a princess somewhere else and try to forget what was going on around me.

My parents finally divorced when I was ten. Divorcing definitely didn't stop the anger and fighting. It was clear, in my mind, that my parents hated each other. My father said the cruelest things to me about my mother. He told me, daily, how horrible she was. She was a liar, a thief, an adulterer and that my brother and I would be forced to live in poverty because of her "sins." The truth is that not one of those descriptions of my mother was accurate. My father's words were only words he used trying to mend his own broken spirit. She was a beautiful, faithful, and devoted wife. But, the truth didn't matter when every day you are told the opposite.

Mom decided she wasn't going to talk bad about our father. Instead she would say things like "I loved him so much. I tried so hard to change him with love," or "I begged him to love me and prayed everyday he could change." I was aware when she told him our water heater was busted, so he held his child support longer to make her suffer. Even though she tried her hardest to not talk bad about him, it was clear how she felt about him. More clear than anything was how depressed and miserable she was. She was lethargic and hated herself more than ever. All of this I thought was because of my father.

In all honesty, my parents were both victims of their own upbringing. Neither of them were ever bad people. But, the honesty part didn't matter in my ten-year-old mind. All that mattered at that point in life is that both my parents were miserable and, according to them both, "bad people. " It is hard for a child to grasp the concept of how they are supposedly a good person but their parents are not. If my father is an incorrigible tyrant and my mother is trifling, how am I not these things? I am half my father and half my mother which equates to me being a trifling incorrigible tyrant! So this is the part of the story where I first began covering my crown with mud. Because I was more concerned about my parent's depression than my own, I kept everything that I was feeling inside. I put on a fake smile and lived with my own self-pity and inadequacies.

Because I was a little miss know-it-all, I knew I didn't need to share my feelings. I knew that plenty of kids had problems worse than mine and that I didn't need to bother others with my petty concerns. This grew into my teenage years, which was about the same time my crown started choking me. I was so defiant of what God had blessed me with, what he has blessed us all with, our worthiness. God kept using others to minister to and love me. But my hard head smiled and agreed, but didn't listen to the words. Certainly my crown had dropped around my neck because I was too clueless to pick it up and put it where it belonged.

As a young woman, in my early twenties, I thought I had it all figured out. I had done everything I was "supposed" to do to fix myself and make myself happy. I had worked my way through college, gotten a career I was proud of, and financed my own car and home. But, I was in a relationship I was miserable in and didn't know how to escape. Thanks to his constant talking down to me, I was pretty convinced something was wrong with me and, that even if I left him, I still would be unhappy. I actually believed that maybe he was right. Maybe the trifling, incorrigible tyrant inside of me was the problem. Maybe no relationship, career, or house could make this miserable person happy.

At my breaking point, I did what I always did when I felt hopeless, I went to my childhood home and laid in my brother's childhood room. It had always been my safe place as a child. My brother was my only lifelong friend and always my biggest fan. As I laid in the floor of his room drowning in self-pity, I saw, in his closet, one of my old pageant crowns. I'm sure he had used it as buried treasure in one of his childhood pirate adventures.

So, like a child, I put on this dirty crown and stared in the mirror. I thought about all the good things. I thought about how my step-dad called me princess or pumpkin every day because he loved me. I

remembered my Grandma telling me over and over
how proud she was of me. I knew my brother loved me
because he wanted my advice on everything. My mom
and dad had always told me I was great, and I thought
maybe I am, maybe they weren't wrong. Why did I
always doubt myself so? Then I heard the words I had
been told one of the times that I wasn't listening. I
heard my aunt's voice loudly say "you are the daughter
of the most high God!"

My emotions took over and those words hit me
like a ton of bricks. I am the daughter of the most high
God! This was the day I finally put my crown back on
my head. God gave me that crown, how dare I take it
off? How dare I deny what God has given me?
Denying God's love and blessings had made me sad,
inadequate, and missing out on life. That day, when I
decided to claim what God had given me, my life
changed! I was instantly happy. I felt free, a type of
freedom I had never experienced. I stopped being
angry for no reason. I lost my unprovoked stress. In
the following weeks, I lost physical weight and my face
changed in the mirror. My skewed adolescent self-
image had left. Praise the Lord! I was set free by Jesus'
blood, and I found happiness. I kept happiness. I find
so much joy daily in thanking God for my blessings
that I have lost my concern for trivial things.

I only share my story because I hope it may bless
you. I pray that you can see that you, too, can let go of
the past and claim your future. If there is any way to
look inside yourself and understand that your damaged
little girl is not what defines you, I beg you to put on
your crown! Please accept the crown that God has
given you. Please experience his love. You know his

love is there and, like me, you have always known. YOU are the daughter of the most high God! Your father is the King of Kings! You are a princess and heir to his mighty throne. Jesus died so that we may experience the glory of his kingdom. Experience the same freedom and love that has set me free. Pick up your crown, dust it off, and embrace your inner Princess! Yes, you are a Princess.

Revelations 17:14
They will make war on the Lamb, and the Lamb will conquer them, for he is Lord of lords and King of kings, and those with him are called and chosen and faithful."

Notes

On this page take the time to examine how you may relate to the chapter you have just read. How will you be able to utilize the points made in this chapter? How will you apply them to your actions and your daily decisions? In healing, it is so important to stop lying to yourself. Be honest, this is between you and God. Remember God loves you, no matter what you believe. If you will be honest with yourself you will be healed by applying these simple but painful truths to your life. Don't give up push through!

_____

_____

_____

_____

_____

_____

_____

_____

_____

_____

_____

_____

_____

_____

_____

_____

_____

_____

_____

_____

_____

_____

_____

_____

Chapter 13

Take Out the Trash And RE-Write Your Story

By Debra Sutterfield

Whether you think you can or think you can't- you are right!

Henry Ford

It's time to take out the trash. It's hard to live in the present when your mind is living in the past. While living in Sodom, Lot's wife allowed the filth of sin to permeate into her heart and soul. She began to see evil as her friend. The angels of mercy offered to save her, but hanging on to her past was so important she lost everything, just to look back one last time. The angels warned her to not look back, but with her last breath she turned to look and became a pillar of salt. The angels warned Lot and his family "Escape for thy life, look not behind thee" Genesis 19:16. Today, if you listen carefully, God is telling you "remember Lot's wife; don't look back."

You cannot live in prison and be free. You cannot live in your past and not feel the pain. Once that egg is scrambled, it cannot be unscrambled. We cannot change where we have been, but we can change where we are going, but only by looking forward.

Luke 9:62
Jesus replied, "no one who puts a hand to the plow and looks back is fit for service in the kingdom of God."

The reason for Jesus's statement is, if we take our eyes off of where we are headed and look back to where we have been, we will lose our course. We have to keep our head out of the trash heap and keep our eyes on the treasure, the victory, the reward for the battle. Satan has, and will forever try, to keep you in your past. That is the only place he can keep you in complete control, in submission to stinking thinking.

Today let's make a plan, take out the trash, take

160

it to the curb, and spit shine our temple. Let's make room for the God of mercy, salvation, joy, and peace. The Holy Spirit will not live in a negative environment. It may seem like you will never be able to do this, it probably feels as if your trash is impossible to move, but it's not. You can do this! Grab a broom and sweep out your negative words, polish up your heart of forgiveness, light up your spirit of praise. Without your negativity and un-forgiveness, without your anger and pain, there within lies a beautiful and precious jewel ready to sparkle and shine.

So the time has come. It is now time to take out the trash. Are you ready? Are you ready to heal? Are you ready to shine? Are you ready to live? Are you ready to give up your past? Are you ready to cancel the assignment from the curses against you? Are you ready to break the generational curses that have been passed down to you?

Over the past several weeks, we've talked about changing our words. We talked about changing our actions. We talked about leaving negativity. We talked about healing and forgiveness. We have spent a lot of time retraining our thoughts; we have been through a lot of pain. Today, as we look over the rubbish in our life, we realize that the trash pile is filled with junk that doesn't work for anything more than to keep us in a negative environment, right where the enemy wants us to stay.

With all of the ammunition you now have to do battle against Satan, the first thing we need to do is take all of the weapons he has used against us, the entire arsenal, and lay it at the altar. Lay it down at the altar and never, ever look back. Your past does **not** define

161

who you are! Your past can be used to lift and encourage another precious jewel up out of the sand. Your past will never again define who you are now, but where you walked once upon a time. I always refer to my past as "in my last life." But, even if you use the story of your past to encourage others, you will use it to reflect on how, with the proper knowledge and The Word of God, they too, can become victorious as we have. Always know where you are, because you don't live in the past anymore.

At this point you should be feeling victorious. You should be ready to spread your wings and fly. Take your story, share it with others, and introduce them to a Jewels In The Sand group or purchase The Hidden Princess for your friends. Maybe, you feel ready, motivated, encouraged, and empowered to lead a Jewels In The Sand group yourself or assist your group leader. If you have read this book and have no leader or Jewels In The Sand ministry in your area, and feel led to begin one,

please contact

Debra Ann Sutterfield at

info@jewelsinthesand.org

If you wish to make a donation to the ministry or purchase a book for a friend, you can go to

www.jewelsinthesand.org

or:

Jewels In The Sand
PO Box 194
Lexington, Mo 64067

But, you have one last assignment before moving on. It's time to write your own story. In the first chapter of this book, you were asked to write down describing words as you saw yourself. Today, I am going to ask you to reexamine yourself.

Your Story

Write the events and your beliefs of why you were walking in oppression, who was (were) the key influences for these thoughts?

_____
_____
_____
_____
_____
_____
_____
_____
_____
_____
_____
_____
_____
_____
_____
_____
_____
_____

What were the lowest points in your life? What were your thoughts at these times?

_____
_____
_____
_____
_____
_____
_____
_____
_____
_____
_____

What changes did you make to find victory? What encouraged you to make the changes?

_____
_____
_____
_____
_____
_____
_____
_____
_____
_____
_____
_____
_____
_____
_____
_____
_____

How have these changes affected your life, your children's life, your parents, siblings etc.?

_____
_____
_____
_____
_____
_____
_____
_____
_____
_____
_____
_____
_____

What would you suggest to others who are living a life of defeat?

_____
_____
_____
_____
_____
_____
_____

Today are you willing to assist and encourage others to find victory and freedom from oppression?

_____
_____
_____
_____
_____

Have you reached a place where you realize your happiness is a choice? Knowing this, have you made the choice to be happy and release blaming others for your emotions?

_____

_____

_____

_____

_____

_____

Describe yourself with the words you now see in you. Look back at how you felt about yourself before the group and how you feel today.

_____

_____

_____

_____

_____

_____

_____

_____

_____

_____

_____

_____

_____

_____

_____

_____

_____

_____

If you never knew Jesus before but would now like to have him in your heart, it is a simple thing.

Say the words "Jesus, I am a sinner. I have sinned against you and against others. Please forgive me and come into my heart. I want you to be my Lord and Savior. I know that you died on the cross for my sins and was raised that I might be saved."

If you repeated these words then you may know that you have eternal life. Please get in a Bible based church and begin your new birth in victory today.

Today is your new birthday _____

Month/Day/Year

Welcome to my family, the family of God!

We will often slip back into our past, but it is imperative to refocus on our new freedom quickly so we do not get comfortable in that old way of life again. Meanwhile, celebrate, scream loudly, and proudly, "I Am The Daughter Of The Most High God! By The Blood I Have Been Saved!"

God Bless you and prosper you. Go witness and lead others to Him in victory.

Put on your crown.

You have found the hidden Princess.

www.ingramcontent.com/pod-product-compliance
Lightning Source LLC
Chambersburg PA
CBHW060245050426
42448CB00009B/1576